THE SHAPE OF THE CHURCH

The Shape of the Church

The Seven Dimensions of Ecclesial Wholeness

EPHREM ARCEMENT

WIPF & STOCK · Eugene, Oregon

THE SHAPE OF THE CHURCH
The Seven Dimensions of Ecclesial Wholeness

Copyright © 2024 Ephrem Arcement. All rights reserved. Except for brief quotations in critical publications or reviews, no part of this book may be reproduced in any manner without prior written permission from the publisher. Write: Permissions, Wipf and Stock Publishers, 199 W. 8th Ave., Suite 3, Eugene, OR 97401.

Wipf & Stock
An Imprint of Wipf and Stock Publishers
199 W. 8th Ave., Suite 3
Eugene, OR 97401

www.wipfandstock.com

PAPERBACK ISBN: 979-8-3852-1738-0
HARDCOVER ISBN: 979-8-3852-1739-7
EBOOK ISBN: 979-8-3852-1740-3

10/01/24

Scripture texts in this work are take from:

New Revised Standard Version Updated Edition [NRSVUE] (BibleGateway.com)
New American Bible Revised Edition [NABRE] (BibleGateway.com)
The New Jerusalem Bible [NJB] (Garden City, NY: Doubleday, 1985)

To Rev. Dr. Mara Lief Crabtree
(1946–2023)
for showing me what integral wholeness looks like.

In omnibus autem patribus relucet totum.

(In each part shines the whole.)

—Nicholas of Cusa

Contents

List of Illustrations | viii

Preface | ix

Acknowledgements | xv

Introduction: A Multidimensional Church | xvii

CHAPTER 1
 The Church of Proclamation and Witness:
 The Evangelical Dimension | 1

CHAPTER 2
 The Church Sanctified and Empowered:
 The Pentecostal Dimension | 22

CHAPTER 3
 The Church at Worship in a Symbolic World:
 The Sacramental Dimension | 48

CHAPTER 4
 The Mind of the Church: The Intellectual Dimension | 71

CHAPTER 5
 The Heart of the Church: The Mystical Dimension | 94

CHAPTER 6
 A Church of Charitable Concern: The Pastoral Dimension | 115

CHAPTER 7
 The Conscience of the Church: The Prophetic Dimension | 131

CHAPTER 8
 An Integral Church | 147

Bibliography | 157

Index | 161

List of Illustrations

Integral Perspective of the Seven Dimensions of Ecclesial Wholeness | xxiii

Phenomenological Perspective of the Seven Dimensions of Ecclesial Wholeness | xxiv

Preface

November 3, 1990 was the day I first realized what a tremendous gift an ecclesial tradition different from my own could be. It happened on a charter bus on the way home from a high school band festival somewhere on I-10 East in south Louisiana. The night had long settled in, and most of my exhausted bandmates on the bus were asleep. The languid atmosphere provided an ideal setting for the intimate conversation which was about to ensue between me and my friend sitting on my left. Largely nominally Roman Catholic (I did attend Mass weekly), sixteen years old, and in desperate need of a spiritual awakening to help get me through the rest of my teenage years, my anything-but-nominal Baptist friend and I found ourselves in a deep discussion about God. I remember nearly nothing about the details of our conversation. What I will never forget is the experience of God I had while my friend shared his understanding of the gospel. Overcome with the sense of God's presence, my body began to tremble in my seat. It was as if I was being shaken awake from a lifetime of slumber. The dam in my soul which kept me trapped in my ignorant isolation had finally been breached. The peace of God flooded me, and I realized in one decisive moment what it meant to be loved by God. It was the moment of my spiritual awakening and the source of inspiration that would lead me to spend my life searching for more of the One who on that quiet night on a bus called my name.

My search led me in my early college years away from Roman Catholicism and into various evangelical and charismatic churches, then an evangelical, charismatic bible school in Dallas, TX, and finally to an evangelical, charismatic divinity school in Virginia Beach. My spiritual life was flourishing, and I knew firsthand the inestimable gift of these two ecclesial dimensions (i.e. the evangelical and pentecostal). Because so much spiritual vitality was mediated to me through these particular dimensions and because I hadn't experienced this spiritual vitality in Catholicism, I began to critically evaluate the shortcomings of my earlier Roman Catholic experience. I judged Catholicism as a lifeless relic whose sacramental and liturgical structure perpetuated form at the expense of spirit. Later, I would realize just how enriching the sacramental and liturgical dimensions of Catholicism actually can be when integrated with the evangelical and pentecostal dimensions and that my criticism was really being leveled at the basic problem facing all expressions of Christianity: an imbalanced spirituality operating from only a few ecclesial dimensions to the neglect of others.

This imbalance further revealed itself to me in my mid-twenties after spending several years in the evangelical, charismatic world. My experience of the emotional manipulation and ego-centrism of some of its leaders was taking its toll. On one of my first Sundays after moving to Virginia Beach and looking for a church home, I decided to attend one of the large non-denominational mega-churches in the city. As the service got underway, with music blaring as at a rock concert and worship leaders singing on stage with their images projected onto jumbotrons, I was overcome with how inauthentic this experience seemed. I couldn't take it any longer and got up from my seat and left.

An acquaintance from the divinity school mentioned that he attended a Presbyterian church which he described as being both traditional and charismatic. I noticed it on the way to the mega-church. So, after leaving the mega-church a bit disgusted and longing for a more authentic worship experience, I decided to stop by and check it out. This was my first experience in a mainline Protestant church. The blending of traditional and contemporary expressions of worship; a service with liturgical form yet with some freedom and spontaneity; the recitation of the Apostles' Creed and vestments; dynamic preaching; an orchestra and not a "rock band;" some with hands in the air, some not; time for quiet reflection as well as jubilant praise . . . this experience opened up for me a new vision of what church could be. It was evangelical, it was charismatic, it was liturgical, it was sacramental. What moved me so intensely was the breadth of the experience of God that was mediated to me through all of these ecclesial dimensions coming together in one, integrated moment of worship.

As my first semester of divinity school got underway, I was struck by the diversity of its faculty. Nearly all the major denominations of Protestant Christianity were represented. There was one in particular, though, that caught my attention most of all. She was an Episcopal priest. A quality of presence unlike anything I had experienced in leaders of the ecclesial traditions with which I was thus far familiar emitted from her. It was alluring. She taught courses in spirituality and spiritual formation. I would come to better understand where this presence came from after taking her courses. She introduced me, and all her students, to a spiritual dimension which most in the evangelical, charismatic world either knew little about or overtly resisted: the contemplative/mystical dimension. I began to realize that her self-possession and presence had a great deal to do with this particular dimension which was so apparent in her life. But even more than this, I was struck by how this single individual could hold so many dimensions of spirituality together in herself. To the extent that I even knew about the contemplative and mystical dimensions of spirituality (which wasn't much), I saw them as a contradiction to the evangelical and charismatic dimensions. My Episcopal professor challenged these presuppositions without saying a word. To me, her life was an attestation to the fruit of complementarity and integration. My either/or consciousness was exposed and the path to integration opened up before me.

Divinity school also showed me another ecclesial dimension that my limited experience of church thus far neglected: the intellectual dimension. For the first time in my life, I was introduced to serious biblical exegesis and the study of theology. There is no doubt that there exists an anti-intellectual bias in some segments of Christianity. Operating from an either/or consciousness (an approach for many people of faith, especially since the Enlightenment), faith can feel threatened by a more scientific and rational approach to God. Or, from an integral, both/and consciousness, I began to see, it can be emboldened.

My exposure to the contemplative/mystical dimension of spirituality along with my blossoming theological mind, and the overall integrating movement of my spiritual life, caused me to radically rethink my vocation in life. I began to discover that at heart I was a contemplative who found greatest fulfillment in solitude, but I was also still quite evangelical and charismatic who now was beginning to flourish in the intellectual pursuit of God. I was also gaining a new appreciation for the sacramental and liturgical world of my childhood that I left behind several years previously. Where could I now go and what kind of life would nurture such a kind of mix? That was when the most insane thought crossed my mind: maybe I should return to the Roman Catholic Church and become a monk! But I wasn't even sure if monks still existed. And weren't monks solely contemplative, cut off from the world? How would the other spiritual dimensions in my life be nurtured in such a context? This is when I discovered the person who helped me answer these questions—a convert to Catholicism and monk himself and one of the great integral figures of the twentieth century, Thomas Merton.

I began reading Merton after my first visit to Saint Joseph Abbey, a Benedictine monastery in Louisiana about forty miles north of New Orleans. The vocation director there gave me a couple of Merton books which were being sold at a used book sale. From the moment I began reading Merton, I was captivated. Besides being struck by the spiritual wisdom he so effectively communicated, I saw so much of myself, and who I aspired to be, in Merton. The paradox of Merton's life (and there were many), was that while a monk living behind the walls of a very strict enclosure he accomplished so much with his life. He possessed a special grace to hold so many diverse dimensions within himself: contemplative; monk; priest; writer; poet; intellectual; ecumenist; social critic; mentor. His capacity to hold all these worlds together, I noticed, was what made him stand so much taller than other Christian leaders of his day.

Merton's life also attests to one other spiritual dimension that began to reveal itself to me the more I got to know him. Perhaps the greatest paradox of his life was that his solitude would burst forth in the prophetic cry for justice and peace as it did. Merton came to understand his world of silence as a world percolating with prophetic intuitions. His powerful pen would give expression to these prophetic words born out of his hiddenness with God. There was a particular power to these words that, he knew, could come from no other place but the ground of his own inner poverty. Merton left the world to become a monk for the world, and his silence was turned into prophetic proclamation.

With the help of Merton, I found my vocation in monastic life and entered that Benedictine monastery in south Louisiana, where I spent over a decade of my life. With me I took all my eclectic experiences of God and have treasured them for the integral part they have continued to play in my life. They shape who I am as a Christian, who now finds his home in the Anglican tradition of monasticism. After nearly fifteen years living according to the monastic way of life where my primary duty is to listen, read, and contemplate God and the world around me, I have come to see that one of the basic sicknesses that plagues both individual Christians and the church as a whole is the way we compartmentalize and become entrapped in little enclaves of what it means to be church. What we live may be church, but it is all too often a version of church that is too small and one-dimensional. In our insecurities we try to defend our version of the church, which in essence is just a limited mix of the fuller expanse and multi-dimensional catholicity of the church, and end up closing ourselves off to the possibility of further wholeness. What I hope to contribute in this book is a vision of what the church can be if we put our prejudices aside and see that only in the embrace of the other as gift can we finally realize the full capacity of what it means to be church in all her multi-dimensionality.

Acknowledgements

A host of faithful Christians who have accompanied me along my spiritual journey have inspired various aspects of this book. First, my parents Warren and Nancy Arcement who grounded me in the Roman Catholicism of my childhood. Second, Chris Authement who first shared with me the gospel in a way that I could understand it. Third, the communities of Victory Life Church in Lockport, Louisiana and Christ for the Nations Institute in Dallas, Texas who nurtured me in the life of the Spirit. Fourth, the Rev. Dr. Mara Crabtree of Regent University in Virginia Beach, VA for first showing me what integral wholeness looks like. Fifth, my seminary formation at St. Joseph Seminary College in St. Benedict, Louisiana and Notre Dame Seminary in New Orleans, Louisiana which immersed me in the world of serious philosophical and theological reflection and grounded them in the life of prayer and pastoral service. Sixth, for the community of Benedictine monks of St. Joseph Abbey in St. Benedict, Louisiana for providing me a way of life where integral wholeness could be lived in such an enriching way, and for my students at St. Joseph Seminary College in whose classes the seven dimensions first coalesced. Seventh, for the community of Anglican Benedictine monks of Holy Cross Monastery in West Park, New York for receiving me into this community where I now continue my journey toward greater integral wholeness.

    I would especially like to acknowledge Br. Francis Beckham, OHC who helped me with the illustrations and Fr. James Hess, O.Carm. who graciously read through the manuscript and offered helpful suggestions and encouragement.

Introduction
A Multidimensional Church

This book is based on three foundational premises. The first is that the church, throughout its history, has taken on various shapes depending upon both its self-understanding and its historical situation. The church hasn't always understood herself in one monolithic sense and has grown to identify aspects of herself through her own developmental history. And it was precisely through her historical unfolding, mainly through her struggles, that she has come to discover aspects of herself lying hitherto dormant.

The second basic premise is that it is better to understand the church as having one, integral spirituality, not many disparate ones. This one ecclesial spirituality, though, is best conceived of as having several dimensions which give the church its particular shape at any given time. In the course of the church's two-thousand year history, many ecclesial shapes have existed, some healthier and more whole than others.

A third basic premise follows: God has called the church to wholeness. This book is grounded in this core conviction and is born out of the often painful realization that the church has failed, and, in many ways, continues to fail, to live up to this call to wholeness.

The church is called to wholeness in two primary ways: in its *scope* and in its *internal integrity*. That is, it is called to live up to its mark of catholicity, embracing the whole of its multidimensional fullness which is aimed at expanding its existing wholeness through radical inclusivity.[1] But the church's wholeness is also demonstrated in the way that it is called to be a

---

1. For a helpful treatment of the term *catholicity*, see Delio's *Making All Things New: Catholicity, Cosmology, Consciousness*. Delio writes, "…catholicity is awareness of the whole that moves one to act toward wholeness or unity" (12).

INTRODUCTION

healthy and vibrant community, bearing abundantly the fruits of life in the Spirit. A further conviction of this book is that it is only to the extent that the first meaning of the church's wholeness is lived, its catholic scope, that the second meaning of its integrity and proper functioning can be realized as it should in all its potential. The church is whole that it may be whole. It is only to the extent that all of its dimensions are active and well-integrated that the church can fully be church.

Several books published in the past several decades have examined various models, marks, and images of the church which have offered revealing insight into the church's nature and purpose and have helped chart a path for its further realization in the full breadth of its catholicity. Avery Dulles' *Models of the Church*, which first appeared in 1974, is among the most notable. Our look at the church intends to chart a slightly different course from Dulles' rightly celebrated study. The focus here is somewhat more limited in scope. Rather than examining the church in its totality, it is the inner life of the church, its spirituality, that will be the specific topic of inquiry. Another book, Richard Foster's *Streams of Living Water: Celebrating the Great Traditions of Christian Faith*, first appearing in 1998, more specifically concentrates on the spiritual dimensions of the church. Besides diverging slightly from Foster's six "streams," our approach will more intentionally focus on the integral nature of the church's spirituality . . . on the interdependence of the streams. Ours is properly a book on *ecclesial spirituality* and *catholicity*. The interest is in examining the animating forces of the community of those who have faith in Christ and showing how these forces *working integrally together* take shape—how they inspire and motivate as they do. The institutional dimension of the church will only come into purview to the extent that it helps elucidate the proper relationship between the internal and external, governing dimension of the church.

As there are different *models* of the church (e.g. according to Dulles: Mystical Communion, Sacrament, Servant, Herald, Institution, Community of Disciples), and different *marks* of the church (e.g. One, Holy, Catholic, Apostolic), and different *images* of the church (e.g. Body of Christ, Temple of the Holy Spirit, People of God, Communion), so there are different *spiritual dimensions* of the church (Foster's six "streams" are the Contemplative, the Holiness, the Charismatic, the Social Justice, the Evangelical, and the Incarnational).

Seven ecclesial dimensions will be presented in this study. There may be more or fewer, depending on one's rendering or classification of

INTRODUCTION

the dimensions. These particular seven have been chosen out of my own experience, observation, and discernment and are not meant to be constrictive but suggestive to the extent that they help elucidate why the church takes on the peculiar shapes that it does. They are also meant to help us discern shapes that are healthier and more whole than others. Nearly every particular expression (i.e. denominations and ecclesial communities) of the church contains all seven dimensions which animate its life and give it its shape. But some dimensions are so underdeveloped or overemphasized as to make that particular ecclesial expression unbalanced, at best, unhealthy or even toxic, at worst. No particular shape of the dimensions has ever, or will ever, be a perfect expression of what it means to be church. The church is a pilgrim church on the way toward wholeness . . . and will always be. But thanks, in large part to the ecumenical movement of the twentieth century and the general openness, tolerance, and connectedness of the contemporary world, the various ecclesial denominations and communities worldwide find themselves facing new possibilities for realizing true catholicity and wholeness in ways heretofore unseen.

The seven dimensions of the church that will form the basis of our study are:

1. *The Evangelical Dimension*
2. *The Pentecostal Dimension*
3. *The Sacramental Dimension*
4. *The Intellectual Dimension*
5. *The Mystical Dimension*
6. *The Pastoral Dimension*
7. *The Prophetic Dimension*

Viewed phenomenologically, the evangelical, pentecostal, and sacramental dimensions can be considered the *dimensions of initiation*. Individual Christians and communities together are initiated into the life of Christ through hearing and believing the gospel, receiving the Holy Spirit, and participating in the sacraments of Baptism and Eucharist. Each of these dimensions continue to perdure in the life of the church and should always be understood as dynamic, generative realities, never static, sterile ones from which we eventually graduate. These three dimensions of initiation are perhaps the easiest to identify and some have seen the church exclusively in

INTRODUCTION

these terms.2 But the full dimensionality of the church extends far beyond the dimensions of initiation, and if we limit our ecclesiology to these three alone, we neglect much of the church's vitality, wholeness, and potential for growth and maturation. Following the three dimensions of initiation, then, are the two *dimensions of maturation*: the intellectual and mystical dimensions. Having been initiated into the life of Christ, engaging the dimensions of the mind and heart are the way that the church matures into the full stature of Christ, understanding with spiritual insight and wisdom and knowing through intuition and contemplation.

Finally, the church is led to engage the *dimensions of ministry*: the pastoral and prophetic dimensions. Alive in Christ, the church acts as Christ acts—through its pastoral service of care and compassion and by bearing prophetic witness to justice and truth. Love and light are the predominant symbols of these dimensions: love (pastoral dimension) which is the primary fruit of the Spirit and light (prophetic dimension) which shines in the darkness and overcomes it. The dimensions of maturation and ministry, it should be noted, are present in every Christian no matter how newly initiated but come to full flower only through the process of their being nurtured over time. It is crucially important to see that each dimension is already present from the moment of the church's conception (and in each individual Christian in it) ready to be engaged, nurtured, and put into practice. If the work of the church is the same work of Christ—*to reconcile the world to God*—then the work of the church must engage all of its God-given potential for the realization of this work. It must be fully dimensional in its scope and internal integrity.

A *dimension* can be defined as an aspect or feature of a particular thing. By referring to the *dimensions of the church*, we mean to highlight the various aspects or features of the inner life of the church that constitute the church as church—that make up the church's soul, as it were. As a study in *integral* ecclesial spirituality, we mean to highlight that no dimension can or ought to exist in isolation but is inherently constituted toward the other dimensions and finds its fulfillment only when functioning interdependently with them. Notably, such interdependence was also an aspect of Dulles' models, though less emphasized as here.

Each ecclesial dimension bears with it a particular gift to the overall shape of the church, but each dimension also bears with it debilitating

---

2. Smith, *Evangelical, Sacramental, and Pentecostal: Why the Church Should Be All Three*.

possibilities if it dominates and is not properly integrated with the other dimensions. It will be necessary, then, to make certain prognoses on particular expressions of the church based on the shape of its catholicity and internal integrity (or lack thereof). These prognoses will certainly not be strictly based along denominational lines—there are healthy and unhealthy expressions of ecclesial spirituality in every Christian denomination. The goal is to utilize the seven dimensions as a compass and gauge to chart our way toward developing healthier ecclesial communities and guarding against the imbalances and extremes that can so easily beset communities as they seek to grow toward spiritual maturity.

Each chapter will highlight each individual dimension but always with an eye on its integral position within the whole. The first task will be to ground each dimension in Sacred Scripture. From this grounding, basic characteristics of the dimensions will be ascertained and investigated. The particular gifts that each dimension offers to the church as a whole will be noted, and attention will be given to the particular problems that arise when each dimension is either overemphasized or neglected. Examples of individuals and movements that best embody the given dimension will be offered to help illustrate our assessment. Non-integral examples will also be presented to demonstrate what the church looks like when it is out of shape.

Each chapter will also balance this synchronic approach by diachronically charting how the seven spiritual dimensions developed and took particular shapes throughout the history of Christianity. Beginning with Sacred Scripture, we will see how historical circumstance exerted the kind of determination it did on why certain dimensions came to be emphasized as they had and why some de-emphasized. What will become obvious is that the driving force behind nearly every reform movement in the church has been the fact that certain dimensions lied dormant and needed to be re-integrated into the whole. A typical phenomenon often then followed: the overemphasis of the dimension(s) neglected in the process of reintegration and a resulting imbalance of ecclesial spirituality, with the church's catholicity compromised as a result. Looking back at the church's history, we see a constant swinging of the spiritual pendulum where reaction after reaction ends up determining often hundreds of years of ecclesial identity and has frequently given birth to new ecclesial movements which define themselves largely along the church's once neglected but now resurrected spiritual dimension(s)—but often at the price of the church's catholicity.

INTRODUCTION

What will come into focus by the end of our journey will be an honest assessment of where the church finds herself in these early years of the twenty-first century—how we got here—and, more importantly—how to face our future more judiciously by learning from our past. Knowing who we are as church and how we grow and thrive as church will form the building blocks for constructing a hopeful vision of what we are truly called to be as church.

Evangelical

Prophetic   *Pentecostal*

HOLY
Pastoral   TRINITY   *Sacramental*

Mystical   *Intellectual*

**Integral Perspective of the
Seven Dimensions of Ecclesial Wholeness**

The Holy Trinity of Relational Wholeness is the integrating force—at once centrifugal and centripetal—of the seven dimensions of ecclesial wholeness.

HOLY TRINITY
Relational Wholeness

Dimensions of Initiation

Evangelical

Pentecostal & Sacramental

Dimensions of Maturation

Intellectual & Mystical

Dimensions of Ministration

Pastoral & Prophetic

WORLD
Transfigured by Holy Trinity of Relational Wholeness through the Ecclesial Wholeness of the Church

---

Phenomenological Perspective of the Seven Dimensions of Ecclesial Wholeness

Participation in the life of Christ is like the River of Life (Rev 22:1–2) whose source is the Holy Trinity and whose mission is the full immersion of the world into the Holy Trinity of relational wholeness.

Beginning with our immersion into the life of Christ, we grow in the knowledge and experience of the Holy Trinity as we flow through each of the seven dimensions of ecclesial wholeness, which results in the overflowing of divine life, reconciling the world to God.

CHAPTER 1

The Church of Proclamation and Witness

The Evangelical Dimension

SCRIPTURAL ROOTS

The evangelical dimension of the church finds its genesis in the God who chose not to remain distant and veiled from creation but rather chose freely to enter into it and draw it into a covenantal bond. A God who initiates covenants to a world gone astray constantly on the brink of self-destruction and saves it from itself is a God worth proclaiming. That God intervenes on behalf of humankind is *good news* indeed. That God makes and keeps promises to guide, protect, save, and bless is even better. The evangelical dimension of the church is, thus, founded on the *experience* of the saving power of God and the subsequent *knowledge* of what this experience reveals about the character of this God who saves. But the heart of the evangelical dimension is best captured in the way that the good news of this divine experience and knowledge compels one to proclaim it and share it. The evangelical, then, is the one who bears witness to one's encounter with the living God through word and deed.

The evangelical dimension of the Old Testament took a giant leap forward in its development as this God who makes and keeps promises vulnerably revealed the divine name, *Yahweh*—the God who is and will always be there. The revelation of the sacred name was such a watershed moment in the life of Israel because of the implications such a revelation discloses. The transcendent God above all gods that cannot be imaged does in fact want to be known on the most intimate of terms. This God seeks a relationship—at once as Creator to creature and as King to subject, but also as a Father/Mother to a child or even as a husband to his bride. The God of the Old Testament, thus, in disclosing the divine name takes a risk to be acted upon and rejected, if only that this God may be known—not so much rationally—but through the experience of *hesed,* this God's enduring lovingkindness. It is the name of *this* God that Israel must call upon and proclaim.

The books of the Old Testament present us with a tradition—a passing down, first orally then in written form—of the story of this God of enduring, merciful love. The inspired authors felt compelled to tell the story of a God who intervenes on behalf of a persecuted people and is intimately involved in righting wrong and preserving justice and peace. Yahweh, who is often depicted as exerting divine judgment on Israel and her neighbors, does so because Yahweh is a jealous God who punishes only to save. The ultimate message of the God of the Old Testament is that Israel's God, Yahweh, is a God who saves.

. . . and will save. Israel's prophets bore the evangelical message of justice and salvation that pointed the way to a future hope of a coming reign when righteousness and peace would flow like a river and there would be no more tears or sickness or death. Hope was even embodied as a "servant" and messiah who would vicariously suffer and bring healing and redemption to the abused and persecuted. Yahweh would bring those in exile home and dry bones would revive. The proclamation of a new heaven and a new earth when the Spirit of God would dwell in human hearts gave a suffering and persecuted nation reason to live and imbued tragedy with meaning. Through their suffering, they would bring healing to the nations and become a light to the gentiles.

These messianic prophecies of the Old Testament formed the exegetical core for their interpretation of the life, death, and resurrection of Jesus of Nazareth who the New Testament writers boldly proclaimed as the Christ of God—the fulfillment of all messianic hope. Like the ancient Israelites, their evangelical inspiration came from an experience and the knowledge that this experience conveyed. *The encounter with the presence of Jesus alive after his crucifixion is the heart-beat of the evangelical dimension of the church.* The entirety of Christianity lies in this experience and in its implications. For the early Christians first making sense of their experience of the risen Lord, the Old Testament served as one of the main exegetical tools for constructing their kerygmatic message and realizing the full extent of what God had done, and was doing, through the death and resurrection of Jesus Christ. Of course, the memory of Jesus, his life and teachings, also became an essential part of the gospel message, but it was secondary to the heart of the kerygma which is specifically the message of the death and resurrection of Jesus and the implications of these events for humanity—indeed, for all the created world.

Beginning with Mary Magdalene, the "Apostle to the Apostles," the good news about who Jesus really is began to spread and the gospel moved from being simply the good news about God to including the good news about Jesus. Jesus became the definitive interpretation of the character of God and the all-sufficient content of God's kerygma. The fact that God raised up Jesus from death meant that God had vindicated the one who had been criminally charged as an insurrectionist and blasphemer. In raising Jesus from the dead, God, in effect, proclaims Jesus' executioners guilty and Jesus himself innocent and, thus, God the Father really becomes the first to bear the evangelical message. The Father proclaims in the event of the resurrection of the Son: death has lost its sting and hope beyond hope is our greatest truth. It is the triumph of Spirit over the tyranny of sinful humanity caving in on itself and the transformation of every obstacle into an opportunity for transcendence.

The greatest proclaimer and interpreter, even shaper, of the gospel in the New Testament was Paul of Tarsus. More than any other New Testament figure, he drew forth the full implications of the paschal event of Christ. Several points stand out as central to his understanding of the gospel:

- The gospel is the *power of God* for salvation (Rom 1:16)
- Christ is our *justification, sanctification, and redemption* (1 Cor 1:30)
- God's salvation comes to us freely *by grace* and received without coercion only *through faith* (Rom 3:24)
- Those baptized into Christ are *baptized into his death and resurrection* (Rom 6:3)
- In Christ we become *heirs with him of God's glory* (Rom 8:17)
- *The Spirit of God dwells within us and will raise us from death* just as Jesus was raised from death (Rom 8:11)
- In Christ we are a *new creation* and the old sinful self no longer has tyranny over us (2 Cor 5:17)

> *Nothing can separate us from the love of God* which comes to us in Christ Jesus (Rom 8:39)

In Paul we find the full flowering of the meaning of the Paschal Mystery of Christ which is rightly described as a form of Christ-mysticism. The Christian and the church become mystically the body of Christ, sharers in his life and participators in his life of redemption. Christ is mystically still present on earth through his church sharing the good news of salvation. For Paul, the kerygma is to be incarnated in every dimension of human life and with boldness of spirit, we, in the fullness of being, make known the eternal life that is actually possible in the here and now. In season and in out, we intently become all things to all that all may have an opportunity to share the gospel . . . that God may be all in all.

Writing to the Romans, Paul emphasizes just how much the church is dependent on the evangelical dimension for its internal integrity:

> But what does it say? "The word is near you, in your mouth and in your heart" (that is, the word of faith that we preach), for, if you confess with your mouth that Jesus is Lord and believe in your heart that God raised him from the dead, you will be saved. For one believes with the heart and so is justified, and one confesses with the mouth and so is saved. For the scripture says, "No one who believes in him will be put to shame." For there is no distinction between Jew and Greek; the same Lord is Lord of all, enriching all who call upon him. For "everyone who calls on the name of the Lord will be saved." But how can they call on him in whom they have not believed? And how can they believe in him of whom they have not heard? And how can they hear without someone to preach? And how can people preach unless they are sent? As it is written, "How beautiful are the feet of those who bring the good news!" (NRSVUE, Rom 10:8–15).

The content of the kerygma is nowhere better articulated in the writings of St. Paul than at the end of his first letter to the church in Corinth:

> Now I am reminding you, brothers, of the gospel I preached to you, which you indeed received and in which you also stand. Through it you are also being saved, if you hold fast to the word I preached to you, unless you believed in vain. For I handed on to you as of first importance what I also received: that Christ died for our sins in accordance with the scriptures; that he was buried; that he was raised on the third day in accordance with the scriptures; that he appeared to Cephas, then to the Twelve. After that,

he appeared to more than five hundred brothers at once, most of whom are still living, though some have fallen asleep. After that he appeared to James, then to all the apostles. Last of all, as to one born abnormally, he appeared to me. For I am the least of the apostles, not fit to be called an apostle, because I persecuted the church of God. But by the grace of God I am what I am, and his grace to me has not been ineffective. Indeed, I have toiled harder than all of them; not I, however, but the grace of God [that is] with me. Therefore, whether it be I or they, so we preach and so you believed (NRSVUE, 1 Cor 15:1–11).

By the end of the first century, four accounts of the life, death, and resurrection of Jesus Christ were written and used in the life of the church to pass on the good news. These "Gospels" expanded the core kerygmatic message to include the ministry of Jesus, focusing mainly on his teachings and mighty deeds, in addition to the accounts of his Passion, which were likely the earliest parts of the accounts to have been assembled. Two of these Gospels (Matthew and Luke) also included narrative accounts of Jesus' birth. All four canonical Gospels are interpretive accounts of the meaning of Jesus of Nazareth and thus are intentionally kerygmatic just as St. Paul was, only here in narrative form. The author of the Fourth Gospel ends his account by stating that his reason for writing was "that you may believe that Jesus is the Christ, the Son of God, and that believing you may have life through his name" (NJB, 20:31). By giving us the content of Jesus' message stemming from his ministry, the four Gospels have been an invaluable source in complementing the writings of St. Paul and the other New Testament letters as they sought to pass along the good news to a new generation of Christians. Not only can we proclaim the central kerygmatic event of Jesus' death and resurrection and participate in it through the reception of this kerygma through faith, but, because of the four Gospels, we can hear how Jesus himself proclaimed the good news about God. His central metaphor for this good news was the "kingdom of God" and its imminent presence. This metaphor, of course, would have been readily understood by Jesus' mainly Jewish audience. For Jesus, much like John the Baptist before him, now is the time to repent because the kingdom of God is at hand. God's saving hand is now reaching into the created world to save it in a definitive, decisive way. We'll know the presence of this kingdom and its establishment in our lives when we are free to live in peace and love even with our enemies; when we are free to put ourselves last so that others may be first; when we are free to serve and give of ourselves in an unrelenting manner; when we are free to lay our lives down that others may live—when we are free to live like Jesus lived.

In the Acts of the Apostles, we see the early Christian movement wildly expand through the evangelical witness of those empowered by the Spirit—even in foreign languages! Christ is a message for all peoples, the personification and fulfillment of Israel and her call to be a light to the gentiles. A general pattern of evangelism is established by the author: proclamation of the good news; faithful response; reception of the Holy Spirit (often with accompanying signs) and baptism (i.e. incorporation into the life of the church). By the end of Luke's second volume, the gospel is set to be proclaimed to the ends of the earth and the reader is invited to take over where the Apostles left off and continue their heroic mission to make Christ known to all peoples.

The book of Revelation proclaims in prophetic and apocalyptic symbol God's eschatological triumph over evil, sin, and death in the consummation of all things when God finally becomes all in all. Rhetorically written to encourage hope and endurance amidst persecution, Revelation effectively incites faith and courage through its vision of what is soon to come.

DEFINING CHARACTERISTICS

Several features of the evangelical dimension of the church become evident from this biblical survey:

- The evangelical dimension is centered on the *Word of God*, its proclamation and interpretation.
- The evangelical dimension, to a certain degree, depends on the *integrity of the proclaimer for the effectiveness of the proclamation*.
- The evangelist is one whose *life bears witness* to the gospel one proclaims—their very life is a word of proclamation.
- The *content of the proclamation matters,* for it alone is the message that saves. *The kerygmatic message is specific and concise* and is not a generalized version of the church's beliefs as in a catechism.
- The evangelical dimension emphasizes *continuity of expression* even while it adapts its message to new generations.
- There is a certain *primacy* of the evangelical dimension in the life of the church.

- *The gospel implicates all parts of one's life.*
- The evangelical dimension is inherently *inclined toward mission.*
- The evangelist should *expect to be persecuted* for the gospel.
- The proclamation of the gospel affects a *transformative experience* in those who receive it in faith.
- The word of proclamation is *directed to an eschatological end.*

The evangelical dimension of the church is the *church that communicates*, both carefully and creatively, the saving message of and about Jesus Christ. Central to the evangelical dimension is the Word of God, understood primarily as a living person, Jesus Christ, whose life proclaims the truth of God. This truth is distilled in the pages of the Sacred Scriptures which is rightly also called the Word of God. The Scriptures are, therefore, a living word that speaks with the same power as the living Christ. Two primary approaches are employed by the New Testament evangelists in their communication of the gospel: *preaching* and *teaching*. What the biblical witness suggests of the evangelist is that she or he is one who seeks to accomplish the effective communication of Jesus Christ and his gospel about God—interpreting Christ for whatever audience to whom one preaches or teaches. Christ himself shows us that one effective way of communicating the gospel of God is through story-telling and imagery. St. Paul shows us that another way is in demonstrating the full implications of the gospel for human life through instruction, argumentation, and personal testimony.

Jesus of Nazareth had little tolerance for hypocrites, those who profess one thing but live under the rule of another. This is particularly true for religious leaders whose vocation is to teach and preach the truth about God. Scandal is a serious threat to the dissemination and assimilation of the gospel. The flip side to this truth is that the integrity of one's life gives force to one's proclamation. While history has proven that God can accomplish the divine will through anyone, even an ass (Num 22:22–35), God's preference is clearly to have the human heart and tongue speak as one. It has often been said that "people don't care what you know until they know that you care." This word of wisdom rightly roots the gospel in the human heart rather than the human tongue. "From the fullness of the heart the mouth speaks" (NABRE, Luke 6:45). The integrity of the evangelist is, therefore, crucial to the health of the evangelical dimension of the church.

There is only one gospel of Jesus Christ—only one kerygma from which the evangelist draws life and lives to proclaim. There is only one truth that is the source of salvation. The church from the very beginning, as is attested especially in the New Testament letters, struggled to preserve the truth of the gospel and protect it from distortion. The entirety of church history likewise attests to this same struggle. This was particularly true at one of the greatest crises in the history of Christianity, the Protestant Reformation, in Luther's insistence that the gospel stands or falls on the proper understanding of the doctrine of justification. Whatever one thinks of Martin Luther and his specific viewpoints, there is no denying that the controversy and struggle surrounding his central teachings on the gospel helped to bring the church clarity to the actual content of the kerygma along with a better understanding of its full implications for Christian life and aided in the restoration of the evangelical dimension to its rightful place in the life of the church.

Is it proper to speak of the evangelical dimension enjoying a certain priority among the dimensions of the church? While it is true that all dimensions are integrally united and exist together, the birth of the church first came about and continues to propagate itself first through the proclamation of the gospel and its reception through faith. In this sense, the evangelical dimension of the church is a type of vanguard dimension through which the church expands and establishes itself in new territories.

A contemporary approach to evangelization would rightly emphasize the need for inculturation and would warn against a brazen imposition of one culture's particular appropriation of the gospel upon another culture. Nevertheless, by preserving the kerygmatic essence of the gospel, all cultural ideologies and religious traditions are scrutinized, critiqued, and subjected to the gospel's fundamental truth claims. Resistance will then always likely be a common response to the proclamation of the gospel. At one extreme of the spectrum, some evangelists and evangelical movements are skeptical about inculturation, since they see any translation of the gospel from its first century Mediterranean culture as a compromise and distortion. This can also be said of the established Christianity of any culture (i.e. Eastern Orthodox nationalism, European Catholicism, or German Lutheranism). On the other end of the spectrum, evangelists and evangelical movements without a clear sense of the kerygma can end up acquiescing to cultural and moral relativism or religious syncretism where even polytheistic systems are tolerated.

The gospel of Jesus Christ, therefore, is a call to a radical transformation of life at whatever cost. Through it one encounters the living Christ who demands faith. The faithful acceptance of the gospel leads to an encounter with the risen Lord which transforms the human heart and empowers one to live in the life of Christ and his fidelity to the Father. As is imaged in the baptism which typically follows this experience of conversion, the old self under the power of sin dies and a new self, a new creation, rises into being. The disciple under the power of the gospel, then, learns and grows in his or her new self in Christ and more and more enjoys the peace and joy of life in the Spirit, a life clearly distinct from the life that persisted under the power of sin. The gospel is a seed of divine life which the Christian learns to nurture and whose end is, in the words of St. Paul, aimed at attaining "to the unity of faith and knowledge of the Son of God, to mature manhood, to the extent of the full stature of Christ" (NABRE, Eph 4:13).

THE EVANGELICAL DIMENSION IN CHURCH HISTORY

St. Ignatius of Antioch and the Age of the Martyrs

A clear link from the evangelical ministry of St. Paul and the other Apostles of the New Testament to the church's second century would be the evangelical ministry and witness of Ignatius of Antioch (35–108/140). Nothing is known about Ignatius before he becomes bishop of Antioch, that city's third bishop. During the reign of Trajan (98–117), Ignatius is arrested and sent to Rome to face judgment and, eventually, martyrdom. Today we possess seven letters Ignatius wrote on route to his execution. A frequently noted part of Ignatius' epistolary output is his understanding of the office of the bishop which plays a central role in the life of the local church. The church cannot function, worship, baptize, or celebrate the Eucharist without its bishop. But, for Ignatius, this episcopal emphasis stays clear from veering into any form of incipient clericalism, since it is firmly grounded in the other dimensions of evangelical proclamation and witness and pastoral service.

Ignatius refuses to have the church at Rome interfere at all in his looming martyrdom. A bishop, for Ignatius, is one who lays down his life for his sheep . . . and for his Lord. There is no dissonance between office and spirituality here. In his martyrdom, Ignatius would become a proclamation of the "word of God," a word sounding the Word. Ignatius was fully aware of his role as bishop and what it entailed and saw himself as the presence of God, evidenced in the name he assigns himself in the inscription to his letter to the Ephesians, *Theophoros*—"the God-bearing."

Ignatius' life witnesses to a profound wholeness and integrity—he deeply understood his oneness with God and vehemently insisted on the oneness of the church. This oneness is what made the church whole. He wished the church to be the whole Christ, without compromise—one in faith and love as well as one in spirit and flesh. The church's unity is only fully demonstrated when its flesh suffers as Jesus Christ suffered. Ignatius' sacramental dimension also played a fully integrated role in his spirituality in this regard since it is in the Eucharist, the celebration of the passion of Jesus, that the church finds the medicine for healing its brokenness and creating its unity. For Ignatius, if the church fails to demonstrate this wholeness, his death will have no meaning. So profound is the oneness shared with Christ that Ignatius' own death and the death of Christ seem to be one death. As he is "ground fine by the lions' teeth," he prays he will be "made purest bread for Christ."[1]

St. Ignatius and the martyrs of early Christianity, as well as the martyrs of any period of the church's history, act in a purely and decisively evangelical way when they give up their lives in order to bear witness to their faith in Christ and their union with him. They teach us that allegiance to Christ and the self-denial that discipleship to Christ requires sometimes speak louder than words. There is no doubt that there is at least a significant amount of truth to Tertullian's remark that "the blood of the Christians is a source of new life."[2] This logic leads us to a further truth: that any time we deny ourselves for the love of Christ we become an evangelical witness to the supreme value of the gospel.

St. Augustine of Hippo

While Augustine (354–430), consecrated coadjutor bishop of Hippo Regius in 395 and made bishop thereafter, could be a formidable representative of nearly any of the seven dimensions of the church, so integral and expansive was his genius and influence, it is the evangelical and intellectual dimensions where his influence is most undeniable. The choice to offer Augustine

---

1. Ignatius of Antioch, "The Epistle to the Romans," 86.
2. Tertullian, *Apology*.

as a representative of the evangelical dimension primarily rests upon the monumental significance his conversion experience through his reading of Sacred Scripture has had upon the history of Christianity. Augustine, with St. Paul with whom he had so much in common, is a decisively paradigmatic figure for the evangelical experience and way of life.

The story is familiar: after years of intellectual and spiritual wrestling in search of the truth, Augustine one day finds himself at the point of desperation looking for inner peace and resolve. As he recounts in his *Confessions*, one day, while sitting outdoors with a copy of the Bible in his hand, he hears a child's voice chanting, "take up and read, take up and read" (Latin: *tolle, lege*). He opens to St. Paul's letter to the Romans and reads, ". . . not in reveling and drunkenness, not in illicit sex and licentiousness, not in quarreling and jealousy. Instead, put on the Lord Jesus Christ, and make no provision for the flesh, to gratify its desires" (NRSVUE, Rom 13:13–14). The words cut to the heart and flood Augustine with light and freedom. Shortly thereafter, he is baptized by Ambrose, bishop of Milan.

Central to the significance of Augustine for the history of Christianity is the personal drama of his struggle with the power of sin and the freedom found from this oppressive power through the more liberating power of the gospel. It is a similar drama that would play out in the life of Martin Luther and would become one of the dominating characteristics in the emergent evangelical spirituality of the eighteenth and nineteenth centuries. This strain coming through Paul, then Augustine, then Luther, then into the evangelicalism of the modern period up until the present day is marked by an impotent will to effect change that can only cry out for God's grace and mercy for help. Because this strain is marked by such existential drama, dramatic conversion experiences become the norm and expectation, especially in the evangelical spirituality of Protestantism since the eighteenth century. For many who exist along this trajectory of evangelicalism, pinpointing the time and day of one's conversion experience is a regular practice, often given in the context of "sharing one's testimony." A great deal of this paradigm of spirituality was solidified in the fifth century in the life of a thirty-one-year-old African's restless search for freedom and his later personal testimony shared in his *Confessions*.

Another evangelical characteristic stemming from Augustine and his personal search for liberation must be mentioned: *the emphasis on the individual*. The understandably monumental influence of Augustine's *Confessions* on subsequent Christian spirituality has perhaps distorted the broader, more accurate shape of his overall spirituality. Reading the *Confessions* alone, one may see Augustine as a strict individualist who is only concerned with meeting God within himself where his personal freedom in and with God is all that ultimately matters. This, of course, would be a gross distortion of one who also thought it best to live his Christian life in the context of a community and who envisioned God a Trinity of divine persons in intimate union bonded together in and as Love. Nevertheless, Augustine has been championed by those preoccupied with their own personal salvation and those concerned, perhaps even driven, by the personal salvation of others.

Evangelical Monks

From the fourth through the ninth centuries the church engaged in its first expansive missionary endeavors. The evangelical fire which burned in the hearts of St. Paul, St. Ignatius, and St. Augustine found its way into the hearts of many of the monastic leaders of these centuries inspiring them to take the gospel to new frontiers. This period was inspired in large part by the legendary *Martin of Tours* (d. 397) of the fourth century. This soldier turned monk turned bishop (third bishop of Tours) combined apostolic zeal with monastic longing for God to combat the Arians and establish what is believed to be the first monastery in France, near Poitiers, where he lived for ten years preaching the gospel throughout the countryside. This center of monastic life would attract followers and converts and would become the spiritual engine which would thrust Martin throughout western Gaul on his preaching mission. The extensive legendary material which developed in his wake testifies to the profound influence of his evangelical spirit.

Legend would also develop around another great missionary monk, the fifth century missionary to Ireland, *St. Patrick*. At the age of sixteen, Patrick was taken as a slave by Irish pirates and brought to Ireland where he was held for six years. After escaping, he spent time in France where he studied for a while at Auxerre and is thought to have retreated to Marmoutier Abbey, the Abbey founded by St. Martin in Tours, no doubt receiving inspiration from the spirit of this evangelical monk-saint. He is also thought to have received the tonsure at Lérins Abbey off the southern coast of France before being inspired by a vision to return to Ireland to convert the pagan Celts. Patrick would go back to those who once held him captive and become the first bishop of Armagh and Primate of Ireland. His

Confessio attests to his baptism of thousands, his ordination of priests, and even the conversions of the sons of kings.

In the sixth century, the Irish monk *Columba* (521–597), in his forty-fourth year, with twelve companions, journeyed across the sea landing at Iona where he founded a monastery which would become the base from which an extensive evangelizing mission to the Picts of Northern Scotland would be undertaken. It is said that St. Columba never spent one hour without engaging in study, prayer, or other spiritual practices. Sixth century Ireland also produced *St. Columbanus* (540–615), also known as Columban, who is best known for his missionary zeal in establishing monasteries in the Frankish and Lombard kingdoms, most notably Luxeuil Abbey in present-day France and Bobbio Abbey in present-day Italy.

The end of the sixth century was also the time of mission expansion into Britain when Pope Gregory the Great sent the Benedictine monk *Augustine* (d. 604) to Christianize King Æthelberht and his Kingdom of Kent from Anglo-Saxon paganism. The king was converted and encouraged Augustine and his companions to preach freely in his realm. Many of the king's subjects were also converted and a mass baptism of thousands was held on Christmas Day in 597. Augustine would become the first Archbishop of Canterbury and is known as the "Apostle to the English."

From England in the eighth-century would go forth the Benedictine monk *Boniface* (c. 675–754) to the Germanic parts of the Frankish Empire. He was responsible for spreading the Christian faith to many parts of Germania and was made archbishop of Mainz by Pope Gregory III. This "Apostle to the Germans" was extremely successful in organizing the German church and unifying it with Rome. Boniface, with fifty-three of his companions, was massacred while preparing converts for confirmation during his final mission to the Frisians.

The brothers *Saints Cyril and Methodius*, the ninth century "Apostles to the Slavs," originated from Thessalonica in present-day Greece and brought the gospel to the Danubian Slavs subsequently influencing the religious and cultural life of all Slavic peoples. Translating the Bible into what became known as Old Church Slavonic, inventing a Slavic alphabet based on Greek characters called the Glagolitic alphabet, and worshiping in the vernacular were three evangelical approaches most notable of these two brother-saints.

The Mendicant Movements of the Thirteenth Century

St. Francis of Assisi (1181/1182–1226) and *St. Dominic Guzman* (1170–1221) reimagined a form of monasticism void of a cloister and provided Medieval Christianity its most potent expression of evangelical spirituality and life. Promoting a vowed life according to the evangelical counsels (i.e. poverty, chastity, and obedience), these revolutionaries of ecclesial life sought to give living expression in the thirteenth century just as Jesus of Nazareth and his first disciples did in the first century. St. Francis' emphasis was poverty and the quite literal emulation of the one who had no place to lay his head. St. Dominic's emphasis was preaching the truth of the gospel to those fallen into heresy. Each, in their own way, along with the highly influential movements they left behind, recovered the primitive evangelical impulse that had become largely overshadowed by the medieval church's concern for temporal power and influence. What is highlighted by these evangelical movements is the total integration of the gospel message with life lived. This ideal, while certainly not always maintained, was nevertheless constitutive to the vision of these two integral, medieval saints.

Martin Luther and the Protestant Reformation

Not even the success of the mendicant movements could completely turn back the rising tide of the medieval church's quest of power and influence with its resulting corruption. This, along with novel theological developments and ecclesiastical abuses, gave rise to calls for church reform. The watershed moment of this counter-tide of reform came from the young German Augustinian friar *Martin Luther* (1483–1546). As already mentioned, Luther was highly influenced by St. Augustine's personal, experiential evangelicalism. Like his father in religion, Luther's experience of unmerited grace through the reading of Scripture to assuage a guilty conscience caused by sin, formed the experiential basis and thrust of the Protestant movement. As Protestantism began to spread throughout Western Europe, defining characteristics began to take shape. The authority of the Sacred Scriptures as the sole authority for Christian living and the proclamation of the gospel (mostly interpreted through the lens of St. Paul) formed the basic identifying markers of Protestant life. Luther's sincere desire was to restore the evangelical dimension back into the heart of ecclesial life, since, according to Luther, the church stands or falls on the doctrine of the justification of the sinner through the reception of the gospel by faith. The question becomes, however: did Luther's understandable critique of institutional Catholicism, which he saw as obscuring the gospel, help shape the church into a more integral form by his emphasis on justification? This is a complex question which deserves a nuanced response to be taken up further ahead.

St. Ignatius of Loyola and the Jesuits

In response to Luther and the others who were riding the Protestant wave came an evangelical call within Roman Catholicism itself. This is nowhere more exemplified than in *St. Ignatius of Loyola* (1491–1556), the Basque nobleman converted through reading the story of the life of Christ while convalescing after being injured fighting in the Battle of Pamplona. Within Ignatius was born a driving passion for the imitation of Christ and the spread of the gospel. A man of immense spiritual insight, one of Ignatius' lasting legacies is a thirty-day retreat manual crafted to help the Christian enter prayerfully into the life of Christ so as to put on Christ and undergo a radical transformation of life. These *Spiritual Exercises* would become the enduring source of Jesuit spiritual formation and prove to be a formative source for the larger church as well. The Jesuits would grow to become one of the most powerful and influential entities within Counter-Reformation Catholicism, and this evangelical movement would help bring the gospel to the ends of the earth, often at the price of great personal sacrifice.

The Evangelical Revival: The First Great Awakening

A flourishing of the evangelical spirit occurred during the 1730s and 1740s across Britain and its Thirteen Colonies through the preaching of *George Whitefield* (1714–1770), *John Wesley* (1703–1791), and *Jonathan Edwards* (1703–1758), among others. These preachers gave birth to a new brand of Protestant piety that is considered to be the immediate forerunner to the contemporary evangelical movement today which has established itself globally. This revival theology stressed the personal conversion through a "new birth" at the preaching of the gospel with spontaneous outpourings of the Holy Spirit, in direct imitation of the saving events described in the New Testament's Acts of the Apostles. With this experiential spirituality came the assurance of personal salvation to be with God for eternity in heaven and to escape the quite literal flames of hell. This evangelical movement would prove to have an ecumenical reach affecting both Anglicanism and Protestantism the world over. It would give birth to new ecclesial movements which would become denominations in their own right, and, in the twentieth century, it would leave its mark on Roman Catholicism as well.

Protestant Fundamentalism

Enlightenment rationalism and the modernist movement which gave birth to theological liberalism posed a grave challenge to the wide-spreading evangelical movement. In the nineteenth century, some in the evangelical movement reacted with great force and determination against what they perceived to be the relativizing of Christian doctrine and moral truth. At the heart of the debate was the challenge to a bulwark of Protestant teaching until this time, biblical inerrancy, which the fundamentalists considered to be fundamental to Christian life. Along with biblical inerrancy, these fundamentalists determined other fundamental truths: the literal nature of biblical accounts; the virgin birth; the bodily resurrection and physical return of Christ; the substitutionary atonement of the death of Christ on the cross. For a fundamentalist, one could not be a true Christian without assenting in faith to these fundamental truths of the Bible. Thus the line was drawn and judgment easily discerned . . . and pronounced. This in or out stance would also help give rise to the cultural wars of the twentieth and twenty-first centuries and fuel the political divide as these fundamentalists, most notably Billy Graham, Jerry Falwell, and Pat Robertson in the United States, began to align themselves with Republicanism. This marriage of faith and politics is now at the point of crisis due to the paradoxical and surprising bond between some Christian evangelicals/fundamentalists and Christian nationalism. Would such an alignment have been possible if this movement had been better integrated with the other dimensions of the church?

Contemporary Trends in Evangelicalism

Numerous responses within the evangelical movement have arisen in recent decades to attempt to address its unhealthy, non-integral shape of ecclesial life. One of the earliest and influential has been the community and movement founded by Jim Wallis called *Sojourners*. Since the 1970s,

Wallis has been promoting a new evangelical consciousness characterized by a reassessment of evangelical principles and doctrine with a reimagined application to contemporary forms of sociopolitical engagement that addresses the fuller imperatives of the Gospels. His movement seeks to fill the gaps and expose the lacunae of much of contemporary evangelicalism, especially the concern and active engagement for the poor and other social justice issues, as well as the emphasis on community, in order to authentically bear witness to the claims of faith.

In more recent years other movements have appeared which are substantially reshaping contemporary evangelicalism. Leaders such as Brian McLaren and Rob Bell promote a more inclusive and compassionate form of evangelicalism based on dialogue rather than on proselytizing. This Emergent Church movement within evangelicalism values authenticity and conversation over aggressive apologetics or confrontational evangelism. Its style of worship is best characterized as excessively "low church" as an attempt to make the gospel as relatable as possible—no suits and plenty of creative usages of media. Running parallel to the Emergent Church movement is the more conservative New Calvinism movement. Characterized by a similar style and ministerial approach as the Emergent Church movement, New Calvinism stands closely aligned with traditional Calvinism's emphasis on the sovereign majesty of God and against some of the theological trends of the Emergent Church movement. It is interdenominational with a presence in denominations beyond Presbyterianism. It is currently flourishing in Baptist churches.

Evangelical Catholicism and Orthodoxy

In the ecumenical era, particularly since The Second Vatican Council, walls that have stood for centuries between Catholics and Protestants have largely been destroyed allowing for dialogue and cross pollination. This is surprisingly the case even between evangelicals and Roman Catholics, especially with Catholicism's more conservative wing. Begun in the 1970s, it reached a high point in the signing of the 1994 document *Evangelicals and Catholics Together*, whose purpose was to urge evangelical Protestants and Roman Catholics to come together to bear witness to the gospel to the modern world on the cusp of the third millennium. George Weigel, one of the Roman Catholic signatories of the document, would become an influential voice for evangelical Catholicism emphasizing the need for

Roman Catholics to promote authentic conversion experiences, radical fidelity, loyal discipleship, and courageous evangelization.

It was in 1975 that the phrase the "new evangelization" was introduced to the Roman Catholic world by Pope Paul VI in his apostolic exhortation *Evangelii nuntiandi*. It became a central theme for subsequent Popes, John Paul II and Benedict XVI, and has culminated in the Apostolic Exhortation of Pope Francis, *Evangelii gaudium*. For John Paul II, the "new evangelization" was to be new in ardor, methods, and in expression having the purpose of not only reaching people who have never heard the gospel but to also reintroduce the secularized, once Christian western world to the gospel once again. Pope Francis has not spoken much about this "new evangelization" since *Evangelii gaudium*. Rather, his approach has been more incarnational and, one can argue, more effective. Francis is showing us what the gospel looks like and is authenticating its message by his simple, joyful, and Christ-like way of life. His is not so much an evangelization through indoctrination as much as an evangelization through invitation to a Christ-centered way of life.

Protestant evangelicalism has had less influence on Orthodoxy than on Roman Catholicism. Of note, however, is the Evangelical Orthodox Church, founded in 1979, in large part responding to the Jesus People movement of that era. This synthesis between evangelicals, stemming mostly from the organization Campus Crusade for Christ, with the liturgical and theological tradition of Orthodoxy, currently has a modest presence in North America, Europe, and Africa. Orthodoxy's growth in traditionally evangelical countries like the United States opens further opportunities for Orthodoxy to be influenced by evangelicals and to develop characteristically evangelical features to its overall ecclesial shape.

TOWARD AN INTEGRAL EVANGELICAL ECCLESIAL SHAPE

From this brief historical sketch of the evangelical dimension of the church, integral and non-integral ecclesial shapes come into focus. The church was from the very beginning founded on the proclamation of the gospel. The church had a strong ecclesial shape marked by selfless, often heroic, witness to the unique, saving work of Jesus Christ as the one sent by God to inaugurate God's kingdom on earth. While all of the other dimensions of the church were present from the beginning, the evangelical dimension, as has already been established, enjoyed a vanguard position as the church began to rapidly spread. During the period of the apostolic age until the establishment of Christianity as the official religion of the empire with Constantine in 313, the evangelical dimension retained its vanguard position. It would begin to be eclipsed by other dimensions, however, with the advent of Christendom, when Christianity became united with the power of the court and when the masses had suddenly become, at least nominally, Christian. Isn't the gospel something proclaimed to non-Christians? Suddenly, the persecuted church became the church of the establishment and the evangelical fervor of the first Christians had nowhere to go.

Monasticism finds its roots at this time as it sought to distance itself from this spiritual malaise. The evangelical dimension once again found its footing as the monasteries of the Middle Ages became the evangelical bases for their missionary expansion. The established church, however, remained largely encumbered by the loss of its purpose of sharing the gospel and, as a result, began to turn in on itself. In the wake of the absence of the priority of the evangelical dimension, other dimensions were bound to seek to fill the void. The pentecostal and prophetic dimensions would suffer much during these centuries much like the evangelical, revealing a similar trajectory, and demonstrating how interdependent these particular dimensions are to one another. In its place, the sacramental dimension would begin to flourish and seek to fill the void of evangelical absence and to give the church meaning. This occurred largely in tandem with the church's rapidly increasing temporal and institutional components at the time. Thus, the shape of the church, from the early Medieval period until the time of the Protestant Reformation, suffered from an underdeveloped evangelicalism and a hyper sacramentalism and institutionalism. A type of personality disorder set in in the church at large. It was the monasteries and mendicant orders that preserved a more integral shape of the church and served as a kind of remnant bringing the clear gospel message into subsequent generations.

The Protestant Reformation tried to bring the gospel back to the forefront of ecclesial life and, in fact, did so. Lutheranism and Calvinism did a better job of trying to preserve an integral shape of the church than did the radical reformers who became highly suspicious of all forms of liturgy, sacramentality, and institutionalism. In an effort to correct the imbalance of the ecclesial shape of the Medieval church, these radical reformers created a shape of the church entirely new. Their source and justification, of course, was the Bible, particularly the primitive church ascertained therein, especially in the writings of St. Paul and The Acts of the Apostles. Ignored, or conveniently explained away, was the development of church structure already found in Scripture, what came to be known, and dismissed, as "Early Catholicism." But in the absence of a governing body and the demotion of liturgy and sacraments, the priority of the autonomous individual to govern is emphasized and a sense of community with the whole is compromised. The proliferation of denominationalism would follow as a direct result of this disintegration.

Twentieth-century evangelicalism would remain largely hostile to a developed ecclesial structure, to liturgy, and to sacraments. Fundamentalist strains of evangelicalism would also develop an anti-intellectual bent and suspicion. Thus, for much of the twentieth century Protestant evangelicalism would suffer from an overemphasis of the evangelical dimension to the detriment of most, if not all, of the other dimensions of the church. For many evangelicals, to be a Christian was to be an evangelical, pure and simple. Recent trends within evangelicalism are seeking to bring a greater balance and fullness to this myopic view of what it means to be church.

Yet, this brand of extreme evangelicalism, as it has, and, in some cases, as it continues to distinguish itself from the rest of Christianity that it judges to be compromised in one way or another, has revealed the dangers of going at it alone and neglecting the other ecclesial dimensions constitutive to the church. Without the pentecostal dimension of life in the Spirit, the evangelical becomes a fundamentalist and legalist. Without the sacramental dimension, the evangelical suffers from the lack of the full embodiment of the good news she proclaims. Without the pastoral dimension, the evangelical can all too often use the word as a sword and approach the other not as a person with a unique story and history but as a prize to be won "for the sake of the gospel." Without the intellectual dimension, the evangelical is incapable of discerning the dimensions of meaning and truth to Sacred Scripture and handicaps his or her interpretation and application of the text. Without the mystical dimension, the word remains an idea and not a personal, indwelling presence, and personal growth and transformation is stunted. Without the prophetic dimension, the evangelical finds him/herself in alliance with authority and power oppressing those to whom the gospel is primarily addressed: the poor and oppressed.

The good news is that the ecumenical movement has been a dynamic force against the strains of extreme evangelicalism. Worldwide, ecclesial shapes where the evangelical dimension is underemphasized are becoming more evangelical (I think particularly of Latin America), and ecclesial shapes where the evangelical dimension is overemphasized are finding a new, more life-giving balance (I think of the many Protestant evangelicals now attracted to traditionally Catholic and Orthodox ecclesial emphases, like ritual and liturgy, contemplative prayer and monasticism [e.g. the New Monasticism]). This is good news indeed both for self-identified evangelicals and for those who are just beginning to discover what it means to be evangelical.

CHAPTER 2

The Church Sanctified and Empowered

The Pentecostal Dimension

SCRIPTURAL ROOTS

The Bible begins with the Spirit's creative activity as God breathes life into formless and lifeless primeval matter. As is well known, the Hebrew *ruach*, used here in Genesis, can be translated as either "breath" or "spirit." The word refers to the animating, life-force of God. In the book of Genesis, this animating, life-force of the breath of God is the energy by which the created order springs to life and is thereby sustained. A relationship of dependency is, thus, established in the order of creation. To be is to be pneumatically or to cease to be. The drama that unfolds in the rest of Genesis, indeed, the rest of the Bible, is the struggle to live in dependence upon this life-giving and life-animating force of God. Sin enters the world in the human choice to depend upon one's self in isolation from the Creator and Source of one's existence. The result is a disorientation of life from one's Source and a blinding, and then forgetting, of one's life as contingent upon a loving, life-giving Creator. Also resulting in the absence of the acknowledgement of the Creator is the self assuming the role as supreme initiator attempting to navigate through life on its own but without the power or animating force to do so. Life separated from its Source, then, becomes a struggle to handle life's oppositions. A war within the self ensues between the force of life, now impaired, and death. All of this drama is effectively illustrated in the mythic stories of Adam and Eve, Cain and Abel, and Noah and his sons.

Salvation history, commencing with Abraham and running through the narrative history of Israel, is the meta-narrative of God the Creator wooing creation back into right-relationship so as to reanimate the created order so that it may live in fullness of life as God had originally intended from the beginning. Faith plays a central role in this reconciliation. The created human being must encounter the Source and acknowledge this Source as Supreme. This implies the submission of the self to One other than the self and, thus, the honest acknowledgement of the self's indigence apart from its Source. This act of faith or turning from self to Source is the very act of reanimation of life and blessing.

For the Old Testament, the law given at Sinai resulting in a covenantal bond between law-giver (God) and law-recipient (Israel) was never meant to be understood apart from the animating, life-force of God's Spirit. For Israel, the law was spiritual and life-giving in itself, an instrumental means by which God is reanimating the created order according to righteousness. St. Paul, reflecting on the law, will affirm its spiritual nature quite explicitly, even if he doesn't admit to the law the same power that comes through Christ (cf. Rom 7:14).

The relationship between law and Spirit is most strikingly depicted in the Old Testament's greatest human protagonist, Moses. As Moses receives the law directly from God he is overcome with God's glorious presence as this presence begins to be animated through his own body coruscating from his face. He is thus empowered to become Israel's deliverer and savior, acting as God's representative on Israel's behalf.

The power at work through Moses, as well as the charismatic judges and prophets that follow in his stead, is clearly directed toward salvation. God's presence is a compassionate presence that (God is at pains to convince) can be trusted. Only occasionally is the Spirit depicted outside this motive of salvation and more gratuitously (the story of the bald Elisha, the she-bears, and the teasing children comes to mind!). The predominant image, rather, is God in the midst of Israel tabernacling, and later dwelling in a temple, keeping her safe, with the one stipulation of remaining holy before the Holy Spirit of God's Holy Presence in the Holy of Holies. As long as Israel is faithful to her God, she can expect to be protected by God's saving Presence. Infidelity results in the loss of this powerful protection. This is, of course, the heart of the theology of the deuteronomic history. Theology after the crisis of the exile will offer a severe critique to this retribution theology in the book of Job, and elsewhere, and will help to give birth to

Apocalyptic literature which will expand Israel's vision of God's salvation to include the eschatological destiny of resurrection and an afterlife with God in heavenly glory for eternity as reward for one's fidelity under persecution.

The near identification of Wisdom and the Spirit finds its most illuminating and eloquent expression in the book of Wisdom:

> For in her is a spirit intelligent, holy, unique, manifold, subtle, agile, clear, unstained, certain, never harmful, loving the good, keen, unhampered, beneficent, kindly, firm, secure, tranquil, all-powerful, all-seeing, and pervading all spirits, though they be intelligent, pure and very subtle. For Wisdom is mobile beyond all motion, and she penetrates and pervades all things by reason of her purity. For she is a breath of the might of God and a pure emanation of the glory of the Almighty; therefore nothing defiled can enter into her . . . . Although she is one, she can do all things, and she renews everything while herself perduring; passing into holy souls from age to age, she produces friends of God and prophets . . . . Indeed, she spans the world from end to end mightily and governs all things well (NABRE, 7:22–25, 27; 8:1).

All four evangelists of the Gospels testify to the Spirit's descent upon Jesus at his baptism in dove-like form. For John, the Spirit is said to remain upon him, emphasizing Jesus as the permanent bearer of the Spirit. The dove highlights the new creation God is now enacting; a kingdom of paradisiacal peace. The Spirit is said to drive Jesus into the desert to be tempted by the devil. Jesus resists these temptations, presumably through the power of this Spirit now remaining with him. Afterwards, Jesus, according to Luke, "returned to Galilee in the power of the Spirit" to begin his ministry of preaching and demonstrating the presence of the kingdom of God. In his inaugural sermon in the synagogue at Nazareth, according to Luke, Jesus quotes from the prophet Isaiah: "The Spirit of the Lord is upon me, because he has anointed me to bring glad tidings to the poor. He has sent me to proclaim liberty to captives and recovery of sight to the blind, and to proclaim a year acceptable to the Lord" (NABRE, 4:18–19). These words of Isaiah serve as a mission statement and programmatic prophecy for Jesus' ministry. Especially for Luke, Jesus is God's Spirit-bearer healing, liberating, saving, and blessing.

In the Gospel of John, during the Last Supper Discourse, Jesus informs his disciples that the Father would send another Advocate to be with them always, which he identifies as "the Spirit of truth." The Advocate will come to their aid, never leaving them orphaned and will be the source of union with Jesus and the Father. This same Advocate will also teach them everything they need to know and will be sent from the Father to testify to Jesus and to convict the world of sin. Here in John's Gospel the Spirit is sent as Jesus is lifted up (understood inclusively as on the cross and in his ascension to heaven). In Luke the Spirit is given only after Jesus has ascended to the Father. The glorification of the Son of God and the release of the Spirit are, thereby, inextricably linked for these two evangelists.

The abiding presence of the Spirit, for Jesus, seems to have departed at the moment of his crucifixion as he cries in anguish from the cross, "My God, my God, why have you forsaken me." But the resurrection of Jesus will be God's answer that Jesus was in fact not ultimately forsaken and is now vindicated through the Father's outpouring, uninhibited power, affirming once again, as in his baptism and transfiguration, that he is the beloved of the Father. Jesus' great act of fidelity to the Father accomplishes what Israel proved she was incapable of and inaugurates a new covenantal bond between human and divine now reanimating and transfiguring all of creation.

Of all the colorful characters in The Acts of the Apostles, the Holy Spirit remains the main protagonist throughout. The Spirit is first introduced through a promise of Jesus before his Ascension, which he says will soon come to baptize and empower his Apostles and the other family and friends of Jesus gathered, before they become his witnesses to the ends of the earth. This baptism occurs when they are gathered together on the day of Pentecost. Memorably depicted, a mighty wind and tongues of fire accompany this baptism as the Spirit rests on each one of them. As an effect of this infilling of the Spirit, each begins to speak in different tongues at the Spirit's inspiration, uttering the "mighty acts of God" and, thus, bearing witness to the presence of God and God's all-inclusive invitation to salvation. Luke highlights what Paul will also demonstrate as a predominant effect of the Spirit's infilling: the character of this speech (*parhessia*) is free and bold. The fearlessness of the Apostles' proclamation of the gospel adds power to their witness. Just as Jesus boldly proclaimed the good news of God's coming kingdom, even under great resistance and persecution, so now the Apostles are propelled by his Spirit to go forth in like power and witness (*mártyras*). This intentional parallelism highlights one of Luke's main theological points: it is the same Jesus who was crucified and raised in the Gospel, who is now alive in the power of the Spirit in the life of the church.

The Spirit is also at the center of St. Paul's conceptualization of the Christian life. It is the Spirit's role to liberate the person who is baptized into Christ from the power of sin. The Spirit is the sanctifying and glorifying agent to realize in the Christian God's justifying gift of righteousness. This transforming power acts upon and in the Christian through faith, the trust of the Christian in God's saving power at work in and through Jesus Christ. The Spirit, through faith, overpowers the sinful desires of the flesh and enables the Christian to live according to the Spirit and to enjoy peace. For St. Paul, too, this Spirit is identified as the Spirit of Jesus, since through this Spirit, the Christian becomes a child of God and cries out, "*Abba*, Father!" just as Jesus did.

The Spirit, for St. Paul, also comes bearing gifts (*charisms*) for the building up of the church, which he identifies as the body of Christ. It is the Spirit which serves as the agent of unity in this body and diversity in expression of ministry and charisms. St. Paul lists these spiritual gifts or charisms as *the expression of wisdom, the expression of knowledge, faith, gifts of healing, mighty deeds, prophecy, discernment of spirits, varieties of tongues,* and *the interpretation of tongues*. These spiritual gifts find their value, for St. Paul, mainly in their function of service to the church and must not be used for self-aggrandizement. To do so would betray the gifts' own inner logic and the Spirit inspiring them. So, Paul directs their end to that of love which alone endures, highlighting the temporal conditionality of the charisms as a function for the church to build her up until she becomes mature in love.

In Galatians, Paul speaks of particular "fruits" of the Spirit which become evident in the life of the Christian living according to the Spirit: love; joy; peace; patience; kindness; goodness; faithfulness; gentleness; self-control. For Paul, a life bearing such fruit is what essentially constitutes Christian life against which there is no law. Living in the Spirit is living according to the law of Christ which empowers life in such a way as to be lived as God intended, dead to sin and alive to God, something of which the law of Moses proved incapable of accomplishing.

DEFINING CHARACTERISTICS

From this biblical survey, the following characteristics of the pentecostal dimension of the church become obvious:

- The presence of the Spirit is known mainly by its effects: in *creation* and in *redemption* (re-creation).
- The Spirit is directed toward *salvation*.
- The Spirit *brings order out of chaos*.
- The Spirit is the *Source of life* and acts not only as *Creator* but also as *Sustainer*.
- As such, the Spirit is an *abiding presence of life-giving power*.
- If sin is that which draws us away from God, the Spirit is that which *draws us toward unity with God* and is, thus, a *reconciling agent*.
- *Law and Spirit* are not antagonistic principles but *complementary and interdependent principles*.
- The Spirit is an *accessible Presence*, however *holy*, which seeks to *dwell with those made holy* in order *to guide and protect* them on life's journey.
- As holy, the Spirit *remains transcendent* even while imminent and *can never be coerced or manipulated by human initiative*.
- Wisdom is a personification of Spirit who, like Spirit, is characterized by its ability *to reach universally into all things and all people to become its principle of life*.
- The Spirit is the *initiator and guide*, at times, *driving force*, to human life, sometimes leading into the desert in order *to test one's faith* and resolve.
- As saving Presence, the Spirit is *Advocate* to the person of faith, coming to the aid of the one in need.
- Just because one does not *feel* the Spirit's presence does not mean that the Spirit is absent.
- Nevertheless, once accessed by faith, the Spirit can *encompass the whole person, including the emotions*, which may testify to the Spirit's presence.
- The Spirit blows where the Spirit desires and is *unconstrained in reach*.
- The Spirit *delights in breaking through boundaries* and filling anyone who has faith.

- An *intimate relationship* exists *between the evangelical* dimension *and the pentecostal* dimension of the church.
- The Spirit inspires a *boldness of speech* as the spirit-inspired *fearlessly proclaim the gospel.*
- The Spirit is the *life of Christ* in presence and power *in the life of the Christian.*
- The Spirit is the *power of God to free* the Christian from the power of sin and death.
- The Spirit is the *transforming agent* working in the life of the Christian to make one more and more *Christ-like*. It is thus a *sanctifying* and *glorifying agent* and the source of a *righteous and holy life.*
- The Spirit *bears gifts* helping make the church *mature in Christ.*
- The *charismatic* component of the church is only *one aspect of the pentecostal dimension* of the church and should not be confused with its totality.
- The Spirit *bears fruits* validating its authentic presence.
- Living in the Spirit is the *supreme law* of Christian life.

The pentecostal dimension of the church is the church animated by the Spirit of God. It is the church alive in Christ who is acting in and through the church as "life-giving Spirit." As such, the Spirit is the Source of the church's life and her sustaining power. Before the Spirit was given, humanity struggled in her fidelity to God. In the Spirit's coming, a new power, Christ's own fidelity, is now at work serving as Advocate for those who have turned to God in Christ in faith. Through faith, the church continues to draw life from the Spirit and remains empowered in her fidelity. The choice to turn away from God, however, remains—a choice that results in the loss of the Spirit's empowering presence and the possibility for fidelity and righteousness.

The pentecostal dimension of the church, then, is the church motivated and directed by an inner principle, the law of Christ—a law written on the heart, a heart being transformed by the Spirit's sanctifying presence. Her source of morality and righteousness is fully dependent upon this inner principle of the law of Christ written on the heart. Christian holiness, thus, becomes predominantly an internalized reality which authenticates the Holy Spirit's presence through the Spirit's embodiment. The cultic holiness of the Hebrew liturgical and dietary systems either losses much of its relevance or becomes entirely obsolete. This does not mean that liturgy and abstinence no longer have meaning for the church, they are just now rooted in the Source of the Spirit rather than on prescriptions of the law, a Source, the church is convinced, which is more efficacious in enabling authentic holiness to be lived. Christian holiness is the character of Christian life that is essentially God-like. A life filled with the Holy Spirit is a life lived in the *imago Dei* and the *imago Christi*.

The Spirit offers the Christian a sense of the nearness of God's presence and concern. In so doing, the Spirit offers to the human person something entirely new: a relationship of intimacy with God, often eliciting an affective response from the believer. Foreshadowed in Israel's relationship to the presence of God in the temple, the pentecostal moment allows for God, as Spirit, to become more intimately present while simultaneously maintaining the divine transcendence. In the Holy Spirit, the human family is invited to partake of the divine holiness and transcend its own profane constitution. This is all God's doing at God's initiative, and any manipulation or coercion from human ingenuity proves vain; hence the need for the pentecostal in-breaking of the Holy Spirit into humankind's fragility and brokenness. The Spirit is the action of grace.

The Spirit is, thus, a balm of healing for broken humanity and reveals God as supremely compassionate. Revealed as such in the person of Christ, this same Spirit at work in Christ is now at work in the world through the Spirit-filled church to heal, restore, and bless with its own compassionate hands. This compassionate presence of the Spirit moves in the direction of the poor, the oppressed, and the needy, in search of only a mustard seed of faith in order to unleash its saving power. The church full of the Spirit, then, is a church for the marginalized, ready, even eager, to enter into the dark places of people's lives to bring the light of God's saving presence. As presence, the Spirit is patient, attentive, and fully given over to the other in compassionate concern. The Spirit, like the Son, has a kenotic shape. It finds its own fulfillment in the act of giving itself away in love, an act which renews her energy rather than depletes it. As love, the Spirit forces herself on no one but is gentle and often unassuming, present without needing to make herself felt. She prefers to inspire from within and to be known in those whom she embodies rather than in herself. Yet, when necessary, she can move mountains. She is most gloriously triumphant, though, in the way she is able to tame and transform the unruly, selfish human heart and make it love, like the heart of Christ, without pretense, neediness, or conceit.

The Spirit serves to validate the evangelical message of Christ. Whenever the kerygma is proclaimed, its message and reality are experienced through the Holy Spirit as well as the fearless witness of the one proclaiming. Since the content of the kerygma is the fact of the in-breaking of the kingdom of God in presence and power, it is logical that the message of such power would, in itself, convey its reality. The Word of God becomes the instrument of the Spirit of God's presence and power.

As presence and power, the Spirit liberates the person of faith and bestows her own freedom upon him or her, sharing the Spirit's own divine life with the believer and drawing the believer into the life of the Trinity. The fruits of this divine life begin to become evident in the life of the spiritualized person. They are introduced to the rest of the body of Christ now participating in the same divine reality and are offered gifts for the mutual building up of this body. The evidence that these spiritual gifts are being utilized in their integrity is the love that they engender in the body. Through these gifts, and the love nurtured thereby, the church grows in unity, whose unity becomes the sign of the unity of God. The church empowered by the Spirit, then, has one mandate: to live by this law of love. The good news of the gospel is that this is, in fact, possible by the power of the Holy Spirit.

THE PENTECOSTAL DIMENSION IN CHURCH HISTORY

Montanism

Likely a response to the growing institutionalization and secularization and the general cooling of the spiritual fervor of the apostolic era, the church in the latter half of the second century witnessed *Montanus* commence a pneumatic and apocalyptic movement in the area of Phrygia in Asia Minor. Montanus and his followers expected the Holy Spirit to be poured out upon the church in a new dispensation. The witness of the Spirit's outpouring was particularly evident in the gift of prophecy (the movement referring to themselves as the "New Prophecy") which was characterized by its ecstatic fervor and daring claims to divine inspiration, even possession. After expanding into Roman Africa, the movement won its most important adherent, Tertullian, who had grown disillusioned by what he perceived as the Catholics' increasing laxity in the spiritual disciplines. He condemned the "Psychics," or "animal men," and extolled the members of the Montanist movement he referred to as "Pneumatics" or "Spirit-filled." The movement was reduced to a sect after it began to be maligned as heretical for its rebellion against canonical rules, tenets of the profession of faith, and pastoral office. In the Montanist phenomenon is illustrated the tension that will appear time and again in the history of the church and that will play a formidable role in giving her her particular shape at those moments: the tension between *charism* and *institution*; between spiritual fervor and ecclesial order; between a rigorous idealism and a sober pragmatism. It should be stated at the outset of this historical trajectory that an integral vision views these poles as necessarily oriented toward one another and not opposed. It operates with a both/and, unitive consciousness and not an either/or, dualistic consciousness. As has already begun to be discerned, the temptation in the development of ecclesial movements has always been to overemphasize dimensions that are being neglected at the expense of the dominating dimensions. It has proven a difficult endeavor to live in the tension of these poles.

St. Gregory of Nazianzus and St. Basil of Caesarea

St. Gregory of Nazianzus (c. 329–390) and *St. Basil of Caesarea* (330–379), theologians and friends, developed some of the earliest and most important contributions to the area of pneumatology. They serve as representatives of the theological tradition of the church reflecting on the Holy Spirit and are most significant for developing the theology of the Holy Spirit in regard to the Spirit as *person* and to the Spirit's place in the life of the Trinity. It is of utmost importance to highlight the theological tradition of pneumatology in the discussion of the pentecostal dimension of the church if the church is to be integrally understood. Too often has the intellectual dimension of the Spirit been maligned in favor of a more sentimental and emotive approach. St. Gregory and St. Basil offer us a more integral vision.

Gregory's particular contribution was in the area of the *procession* of the Spirit in attempting to explain the unique relationship of the Spirit to the Godhead: "The Holy Spirit is truly Spirit, coming forth from the Father indeed but not after the manner of the Son, for it is not by generation but by procession, since I must coin a word for the sake of clearness; for neither did the Father cease to be Unbegotten because of His begetting something, nor the Son to be begotten because He is of the Unbegotten (how could that be?), nor is the Spirit changed into Father or Son because He proceeds, or because He is God . . . ."[1] This idea would have tremendous influence on the subsequent theological tradition which sought to understand the work of the Holy Spirit in the life of the Trinity as well as the life of the church. Perhaps Basil's greatest single theological contribution was his insistence on the divinity and consubstantiality of the Holy Spirit with the Father and the Son. Basil solidifies the divinity of the Spirit and the reality of the Trinity in one broad stroke and grounds the church upon these two fundamental doctrines. The theological and spiritual implications of both of these fundamental contributions of Gregory and Basil have been seismic for the church, leaving an indelible mark on the church universal—Catholic, Orthodox, Anglican, Protestant—and demonstrate what is possible when mind and spirit function as one.

St. Anthony of Egypt and the Desert Fathers

The story of *St. Anthony of Egypt* (251–356), considered one of the earliest Desert Fathers, is paradigmatic of the spirituality that flourished in the Egyptian desert in the latter half of the third century, that spread wildly in the fourth century, and subsequently became a formidable movement reaching into the Middle East and Europe. Inspired by the gospel story of the rich young man who asked Jesus how to gain eternal life and who went away with head downcast choosing to remain weighed down by his riches, Anthony, in contrast, was stirred to respond in a decisive and radical way. Giving all of his possessions away to the poor and his sister to the care of nuns, he turns his back to life in the city and finds a new existence away from the Nile in the solitude of the desert where he confronts his own inner demons and grows in profound insight to the ways of the Spirit. What results is a striking wisdom and insight into how the human heart evades the call to holiness. As a result of this knowledge of the self, along with the experience of the clear intuition of the wisdom of the Spirit, Anthony, and the other monks in the desert, offer the church in the city a prophetic witness to what life can be when radically submitted to the call of discipleship.

Rather than offering St. Anthony and the Desert Fathers as representatives of the prophetic dimension of the church, which they certainly were (they were also aligned closely with the mystical and evangelical dimensions), I offer them as a vital example of the pentecostal dimension instead.

1. Gregory of Nazianzus, *Oration 39*.

The prophetic lives they lived came as a result of a more fundamental impulse. It is almost certain that what inspired many, if not most, of those Egyptian city-dwellers to find new life in the desert was the same realities that inspired the Montanists of the century before: the waning of the spiritual vitality of the established church. This only became increasingly more the case with Constantine and the adoption of Christianity as the religion of the empire in 313. More than anything else, the Desert Fathers were fired to maintain a fervent life in the Spirit and resisted anything that would squelch this intensity. In the desert, they created a way of life which gave high premium to disciplines that would assure their spiritual intensity and focus. Their asceticism is famous—in certain cases, even infamous and extreme. But these extremes should not obscure their primary motivation, which was to embrace a way of life absolutely dependent upon the power of the Spirit. Many spiritual renewals within the life of the church throughout the centuries would be inspired by these ancient desert dwellers, as scholars have noted. Some of the most notable have been the *Devotio Moderna* movement of the late fourteenth-century low countries, the Pietists of seventeenth-century Germany, and the Methodist Revival in eighteenth-century England. Their harsh asceticism would, however, also be a source of inspiration for a fair share of Christians disgruntled with the status quo, like the Jansenists of the seventeenth century and the many other rigorist movements throughout church history.

St. Symeon the New Theologian

Considered one of the church's greatest mystics, *St. Symeon the New Theologian* (949–1022), a Byzantine Christian monk, is offered here as a model of the pentecostal dimension because of the profound spiritual experiences he conveys through his writings and what these writings say about his life of union with God in the Holy Spirit, along with the Spirit's relationship to the church. With Symeon we encounter a man suffused with the Holy Spirit who creates a stunningly new way of speaking about life in God. The epithet, "New Theologian," refers to the new way of communicating one's experience of God that came in vogue with Symeon. Here is an apt example:

> One day, as he stood repeating more in his intellect than with his mouth the words, 'God, have mercy upon me, a sinner' (Luke 18:13), suddenly a profuse flood of divine light appeared above him and filled the whole room. As this happened the young man

> lost his bearings, forgetting whether he was in a house or under a roof; for he saw nothing but light around him and did not even know that he stood upon the earth. He had no fear of falling, or awareness of the world, nor did any of those things that beset men and bodily beings enter his mind. Instead he was wholly united to non-material light, so much so that it seemed to him that he himself had been transformed into light. Oblivious of all else, he was filled with tears and with inexpressible joy and gladness. Then his intellect ascended to heaven and beheld another light, more lucid than the first.[2]

Symeon's mysticism is highly kataphatic, focusing on the Spirit as light coming from God to take possession of the one in darkness. It is the same light that appeared on the face of Christ. Symeon is usually very careful about connecting his pneumatology with his Christology. He is more cautious, however, with connecting the Spirit with the sacraments. He certainly did not deny the sacraments, he himself was ordained, but he insisted that the sacraments are empty without the Spirit. The need for spirit-filled officiants of the sacraments is highlighted in this passage which applies to the celebration of the sacred mysteries:

> I found that those who do not honor it above all the world, and regard it a glory, and an honor, and a wealth to worship, to preside at the liturgy, and to be present, such people are not worthy of the immaculate divinity, or worthy of the pleasure, nor the joy, nor any goods of which they will have no part without repentance, if, as we said, they do not learn and acquire everything, and they do not do with zeal everything that my God has said. Let anyone, if God should so order, touch the sacred things with toil, and much fear, and reverence. For it is not permissible for everyone to minister to such things, for ever if one receives every grace of the Spirit, and one is pure of sin from their mother's <womb>, unless it is by God's command and his choice that assures and illuminates their soul with divinity, and inflames their soul with the desire of divine love, then it does not seem to me reasonable for them to minister divine things, and to touch the untouchable and awesome mysteries, to which is fitting glory, and honor, and all worship now and always through all, unto all ages.[3]

---

2. Hayward, C.J.S. "Symeon the New Theologian: On Faith."

3. Symeon the New Theologian, *Divine Eros: Hymns of Saint Symeon the New Theologian*, 132.

St. Symeon's concern here addresses a basic concern which will resurface frequently in the history of the church, a special point of contention at the time of the Protestant Reformation. But it was already an issue at least as early as the fourth century with the Donatist controversy whose constituency held that for the sacraments to be valid the minister of those sacraments had to be free from sin. The ultimate concern of these movements, and individuals who embodied them, was to never allow the institution to stand in the place of authentic spiritual action. History shows that institutional dominance and overcontrol has been a common temptation with spiritually debilitating consequences. The Spirit cannot be denied in the life of the church for long. If suppressed for too long, the Spirit will inevitably erupt in a wave of renewal. This can often be a messy time in the life of the church but a necessary one. An integral church, by nature, would minimize the mess.

Joachim of Fiore

The fascinating Cistercian monk of the twelfth century, *Joachim of Fiore* (1135–1202), was well grounded in the prophetic dimension but is offered here as a representative of the pentecostal dimension because of his unique and influential vision of the spiritual age he prophesied which he believed had begun with St. Benedict of Nursia in the fifth century and that was now, in his day, continuing to be manifested, especially in the lives of monks and contemplatives suffused with the Spirit. Just as there was the age of the Father, identified with the Old Testament period, and the age of the Son, identified with the New Testament period, so now there is the age of the Spirit where the words of Scripture find their deepest, spiritual meaning, when a new age of peace and justice reign, and when the church becomes so spiritual as to make the mediating hierarchy all but obsolete. His controversial vision of a new spiritual age was admired by some (Bonaventure accepted certain aspects of his thought) and refuted by others (Thomas Aquinas harshly criticized him). His vision found fertile ground in the Spiritual Franciscans and the Brethren of the Free Spirit but was never accepted as a compatible vision with the Catholic worldview. But Yves Congar asks, "Has Joachimism ever completely died out? . . . For a very long time renewals in the Church have been linked with the emergence of religious orders, and thus initiatives taken by the Holy Spirit."⁴ Speaking further of Joachim's legacy, Congar extends Joachim's reach quite profoundly:

> He introduced into the history of the world, which was for him, of course, the history of the Church, an eschatology that was characterized by the great novelty of a rule of the inner life and of freedom. Joachim in this way opened the flood-gates to admit what could well become the torrent of human hopes. This could at any time result in social protest, a polarized attempt to reform the Church, or many different searches for freedom and novelty. It could take the form of philosophies of reason, of progress, of the 'spirit'. This has, if fact, frequently happened, in many cases with an explicit reference to Joachim.⁵

Joachim tapped into the deep, spiritual aspirations of the human heart for a realized eschatological utopia in the here and now. His problem was not his prophetic vision per se but in his disassociation of life in the Spirit with the temporal, and all too often, broken ecclesial order, much like Montanus nearly a century before him.

Quakers and Pietists

The marginalization of the institutional component of the church was never as fierce as it came to be with *George Fox* (1624–1691) and the movement he founded, the Society of Friends. Like many new movements within the church, George Fox found his inspiration in a religious experience which would cause him to radically rethink the values and practices of Christian life. Struck by an inner light of God's all-consuming love, Fox interpreted this as an experience open to all people. According to Fox, having this experience of this inner flame was the experience that truly made one a Christian. External worship was not necessary. Sacraments and an ordered ministry were rejected. Even Scripture lost its authoritative position for Christian life. The Holy Spirit was the only rule of life for Fox. Listening for God's word of revelation was the sole Christian practice advocated. Silence was thus a particular emphasis in Quaker meetings. Only those overcome with the Spirit were allowed to speak. Quakers' conviction that all people bear the inner light of God has allowed them to take often heroic stances in the face of societal injustices and has inspired peace initiatives from

---

4. Congar, *I Believe in the Holy Spirit*, 129.
5. Congar, *I Believe in the Holy Spirit*, 129–30.

an ecclesial body rarely seen. In 1947, the Society of Friends received the Nobel Peace Prize for such a witness.

Concern must be expressed, however, with Quakerism's approach to life in the Spirit devoid of ecclesial structure. Perhaps the greatest concern is the way that dependence on the Spirit alone can lead to an over-assurance of one's personal conviction and experience equating it with divine truth with little or no accountability. Who discerns the veracity of such experiences? Or the veracity of words uttered in meetings? Without a theology of the Holy Spirit or ordained ministers to guide, relying solely on the *experience* of the Spirit, are other ecclesial dimensions that serve for ecclesial wholeness unduly neglected?

Pietism finds its roots in a book published in 1675 by the Lutheran theologian *Philipp Jakob Spener* (1635–1705) called *Pia Desideria or Ernest Desire for a Reform of the True Evangelical Church*. As a movement beginning within Lutheranism, it would soon bear influence far beyond its confessional lines, most notably John Wesley and American Revivalism. Congar highlights the dialectical swing of Pietism when he writes, "just as a mysticism based largely on feeling had asserted itself in a climate of dialectical Scholastic theology in the fourteenth and fifteenth centuries, so too did Spener want to go beyond a Lutheran orthodoxy that was too rigidly committed to pure formulae and give new life to the personal experience of faith."[6] The Pietists' marked emphasis on personal experience was a cause for concern by the state-sponsored church who considered its emotional excesses a threat to social order and its focus on religious feeling too much an end in itself. Nevertheless, the Pietist movement witnessed to an internal need of the church that has proven to be an integral part of the pentecostal dimension of the church: the need for Christians to express their spirituality through God-given emotions. Pietism tapped into the need for the church to express itself—in worship, in prayer, in community—and serves as a check on disembodied, over-intellectualized forms of spirituality.

John Wesley

When he was thirty-two years old and already an Anglican cleric, *John Wesley* (1703–1791) sailed, along with his brother Charles, to the New World landing in the colony of Georgia in February 1736. It was on this journey that he encountered the Moravians and their pietistic spirituality whose

---

6. Congar, *I Believe in the Holy Spirit*, 143.

influence upon him would prove to be formidable. It was particularly the Moravians' deep faith and peace amidst the uncertainties and calamities of the voyage that impressed upon Wesley the ineptitude of his own faith. The authenticity and radical personalization of faith witnessed to by the Moravians would profoundly influence Wesley's future theology and spirituality which would find a cohesive expression in the movement he founded: Methodism.

After returning to England disheartened and depressed, Wesley would turn again to the Moravians for inspiration. It was at a Moravian meeting that his celebrated "Aldersgate experience" transpired:

> In the evening I went very unwillingly to a society in Aldersgate Street, where one was reading Luther's Preface to the Epistle to the Romans. About a quarter before nine, while he was describing the change which God works in the heart through faith in Christ, I felt my heart strangely warmed. I felt I did trust in Christ, Christ alone for salvation, and an assurance was given me that he had taken away my sins, even mine, and saved me from the law of sin and death.[7]

This experience of the Spirit giving assurance for one's personal salvation would contribute much to Wesley's theological development, especially in his growing emphasis on free grace, entire sanctification, and perfection, and would indelibly shape the future Holiness movement, charismatic movement, and, to a certain degree, pentecostalism itself, all of which emphasize religious experience as that which demarcates the true Christian from simply the nominal.

St. Seraphim of Sarov

One of the great integral figures of Christianity in the eighteenth and nineteenth centuries was the beloved Orthodox monk *St. Seraphim of Sarov* (1754–1833). Of the many aphorisms that bear witness to the authenticity of his life in the Spirit, this one is perhaps the most famous: "Acquire a peaceful spirit, and around you thousands will be saved." With one short saying, St. Seraphim manages to integrate several dimensions into a holistic vision of Christian life: pentecostal; mystical; pastoral; evangelical; prophetic. This loaded aphorism is expounded in the significant conversation

---

7. Quoted in Dreyer, *The Genesis of Methodism*, 27.

with the pious Orthodox Christian Nicholas Motovilov, which took place in November of 1831. In the course of the conversation, St. Seraphim and Motovilov discuss the aim of Christian life. This questioning leads to an articulation of what can be described as St. Seraphim's fundamental pneumatic orientation:

> 'The Lord has revealed to me,' said the great elder, 'that in your childhood you had a great desire to know the aim of our Christian life, and that you have continually asked many great spiritual persons about it.' I must admit, that from the age of twelve this thought had constantly troubled me. In fact, I had approached many clergy about it, however their answers had not satisfied me. This could not have been known to the elder. 'But no one,' continued St. Seraphim, 'has given you a precise answer. They have said to you: "Go to church, pray to God, do the commandments of God, do good—that is the aim of the Christian life." Some were even indignant with you for being occupied with such profane curiosity and said to you, "Do not seek things which are beyond you." But they did not speak as they should. Now humble Seraphim will explain to you of what this aim really consists. However prayer, fasting, vigil and all the other Christian practices may be, they do not constitute the aim of our Christian life. Although it is true that they serve as the indispensable means of reaching this end, the true aim of our Christian life consists of the *acquisition of the Holy Spirit of God*.'[8]

During the course of the conversation Motovilov is struck by St. Seraphim's transfigured face dazzling with the glory of God. This moment exemplifies the goal of the spiritual life for Orthodox Christianity:

> 'Still,' I replied, 'I do not understand how I can be fully certain of being in the Spirit of God. How can I myself discern His true presence within me?'
> 'I have already told you, friend of God,' Father Seraphim replied, 'that it is very simple, and I have explained to you in detail how people come to be in the Spirit of God, and how His presence within us should be known. What more do you need, my son?'
> 'I need,' I said, 'to understand this completely.'
> Father Seraphim then took me very firmly by the shoulders and said: 'We are both, you and I, in the Spirit of God at this moment, my son. Why do you not look at me?'

---

8. Orthodox Christianity. "Saint Seraphim of Sarov: On the Acquisition of the Holy Spirit."

> 'I cannot look, Father,' I replied, 'because great flashes of lightning are springing from your eyes. Your face shines with more light than the sun, and my eyes ache from the pain.'
>
> 'Don't be frightened, friend of God,' Father Seraphim said. 'You yourself have now become as bright as I am. You are now yourself in the fullness of the Spirit of God: otherwise you would not be able to see me like this.'[9]

The Spirit-possessed, transfigured life, for St. Seraphim and for Orthodoxy at large, is Christianity's *raison d'être*. It is the foundation and spring from which all the dimensions of the church flow. Without it firmly established, the church teeters and loses its proper footing. Firmly rooted and grounded in the Spirit, the Spirit becomes the transforming presence of God leading to doxological communion and living.

Twentieth Century Pentecostalism and the Charismatic Movement

The pentecostal dimension of the church has made its way to center stage in the contemporary church globally. Pentecostalism is the most rapidly growing movement in the church today since its most recent iteration beginning in the early years of the twentieth century. It remains a force with which to be reckoned, with little sign of letting up anytime soon. Although pentecostal denominations have arisen in the wake of the initial outbursts in Topeka, Kansas and Los Angeles, California, pentecostal spirituality has now influenced nearly every Christian denomination in every country around the planet. In addition, it has significantly left its mark on Roman Catholicism, if only marginally affecting Orthodoxy. What are we to make of this staggering phenomenon? What does it say about the nature of the church?

In order to answer these questions, we must first examine the foundations of the movement and note its influences. *Charles Parham* (1873–1929) was the step-son of a daughter of a Methodist circuit rider. He married the daughter of a Quaker. At fifteen Parham was already conducting religious services and soon would enroll at Southwest College in Winfield, Kansas, a school affiliated with the Methodists. He decided to leave college after discerning that the education impeded his ministry and left the Methodists

---

9. Constantine Cavarnos and Mary-Barbara Zeldin, *Modern Orthodox Saints, 5: St. Seraphim of Sarov*, 111–12.

over the way he perceived how their hierarchy impeded divine inspiration. Venturing out on his own, he preached itinerantly along the lines of the holiness movement, which emphasized the teaching of a "second blessing" of sanctification, a subsequent experience after one's initial justification. This would lead quite logically to Parham's eventual emphasis on the baptism of the Holy Spirit as a type of second blessing God wished to bestow on all Christians. Such was his teaching at his newly founded Bethel Bible College in Topeka. Giving his students an opportunity to spend time in a type of in-house retreat at the College, they were charged by Parham to search the scriptures for evidence of this pouring out of the Holy Spirit and to pray. The result was that one of the students, Agnes Ozman, during a worship service held on January 1, 1901, began to speak in tongues after being prayed over.

William J. Seymour (1870–1922) was a student of Charles Parham in Houston who took Parham's pentecostal message of baptism in the Spirit to Los Angeles, where, beginning in 1906, he led the three year Azusa Street Revival. Crowds of up to one-thousand five-hundred packed inside the small Methodist Episcopal Church on Azusa Street each night for revival meetings for these three years becoming the epicenter of the contemporary pentecostal movement.

At the heart of the movement was the literal reading of the Acts of the Apostles with its pattern of prayer, baptism of the Holy Spirit, and charismatic phenomena as evidence of the Spirit's outpouring. The logic was simple: if then, why not now. And so they prayed, and with open and expectant hearts and minds, experienced what they considered as the very same blessing of the Spirit as the early Christians documented in Acts.

There can be little doubt that the rapid spread of pentecostalism and the charismatic movement stemming from it is fulfilling a need in the lives of millions of Christians of every race, culture, and denominational affiliation.[10] In order to identify this need, pentecostalism's emphases should be highlighted:

- Emphasis on the experience of God in the Holy Spirit
- Emphasis on the charismatic gifts, especially speaking in tongues and prophecy

---

10. "The charismatic movement" is a reference to the pentecostal strain existing within mainline Christian denominations.

- Emphasis on emotional expression of spirituality through worship and small group faith sharing
- Emphasis on community
- Emphasis on evangelization
- Emphasis on the Bible

It is also important to highlight what pentecostalism de-emphasizes:

- De-emphasis on formal liturgy
- De-emphasis on sacraments
- De-emphasis on hierarchy
- De-emphasis on theological education (although there are notable exceptions to this, especially in more recent years)

It is also important to highlight the development within pentecostalism and the charismatic movement over the course of this past century. Most notably is the shift of emphasis. Generally speaking, the early movement stressed the charismatic gifts, especially tongues and prophecy, as the sure sign of having received the baptism in the Holy Spirit. In recent years, stress is now placed on the worship experience itself which may or may not lead to the sharing of these charismatic gifts. "Praise and worship" has in recent years officially entered the ecclesiastical lexicon. This experience offers to the worshiper an intimate encounter with the divine that is very difficult to communicate in the context of more formal liturgies. There is also a felt sense of God's presence that is often associated with these worship experiences that enable transformational living to take place. With this, however, can arise an inordinate focus upon the emotional component of faith. What is sometimes sacrificed is significant: the experience of the transcendence of God; a faith life built upon something sturdier than emotions; intellectual nuance and wisdom; a neglect of issues beyond one's spiritual experience and the concern for winning souls, especially the neglect of the issues of social justice. Pentecostal groups today are now noticing some of these areas of negligence and are making attempts to correct them. No doubt this is happening because of the ecumenical scope of this movement which allows for greater cross-pollination between denominations.

THE CHURCH SANCTIFIED AND EMPOWERED

The Second Vatican Council and the Catholic Charismatic Renewal

It is common knowledge that Orthodoxy has regularly criticized Roman Catholicism for neglecting pneumatology in its theological discourse and liturgical practice. Such criticisms were not uncommon from the 'observers' during the Council either. Roman Catholic theologians such as Yves Congar, who was perhaps the most important theologian of the Council and worked tirelessly in promoting a stronger pneumatological presence in its documents, have noted the pneumatological breakthrough which occurred during these pregnant and sometimes volatile years. Congar notes several clarifications and accomplishments of the Council in this regard:

- The pneumatology of the Council is not pneumatocentric. It, rather, speaks of the Spirit as the Spirit of Christ, that which builds up the Body of Christ, that which is the principle of life of that Body, the church, and that which inspires and guides the Tradition.

- Vatican II goes beyond a theology of the church as the Mystical Body of Christ and more broadly demonstrates the Spirit as the animating principle of all aspects of the church in the present moment. The Spirit makes the church a personalizing event which draws all people of faith into the person of Christ.

- The Council emphasized the Spirit in the context of the Trinity and the Trinity's economy of creation and grace. The Spirit draws all people of faith into participation in the life of the Triune God. This is particularly evident in the epicleses of the new Eucharistic prayers.

- The Council placed significant emphasis on the charisms and, in effect, sought to balance the long emphasized institutional dimension with the variety of gifts present in each of the church's members. The Council's call for *aggiornamento* was a call to uncover these charisms neglected for centuries and put them to use once again for the ongoing renewal of the church.

- Along with its emphasis on charisms, the Council also placed emphasis on the church's catholicity. The Spirit alive and active in every local church draws us all together into the church universal through the common sharing of gifts.

- The Council draws attention to the action of the Spirit in the history of the world. "The Dogmatic Constitution on the Church in the Modern World" frequently makes reference to the presence of the Spirit in the unfolding of time and in the renewal of the earth.[11]

Many Roman Catholics see these teachings on the Spirit in the church concretely confirmed in the life of the church with the Catholic Charismatic Renewal beginning in Pittsburgh at Duquesne University in 1967. Since then, the Renewal has brought a spiritual vitality to a multitude of Roman Catholics without the often historical concomitant vilification of hierarchy, institution, or sacraments as often seen in Protestantism. The Renewal has offered the highly structured Roman Catholic Church a greater experience of freedom for its members within this structure. While many charismatic prayer groups and lay communities have arisen since 1967, they have in large part remained adamantly committed to remaining within the folds of Roman Catholicism at large. Those promoters of the Renewal have found creative ways to be both traditionally Roman Catholic and progressively charismatic with little need to justify one over the other. A new generation of Roman Catholics brought up in the milieu of the Renewal is generally happy to exist in a church with both Gregorian chant and "praise and worship;" with both Latin and the vernacular; with both organ and guitar. This is certainly not characteristic of all young Roman Catholics, many who today exhibit a less integral consciousness and outlook, reacting against the charismatic intimacy with God of a previous generation and who now exhibit a strong proclivity toward the experience of the transcendent and holy.

TOWARD AN INTEGRAL PENTECOSTAL ECCLESIAL SHAPE

If the evangelical dimension was the dimension of the church focused upon the Word of God and its proclamation, the pentecostal dimension of the church is the dimension focused on the inspiration of that Word proclaimed. Concomitantly, it is the inspiration of all the other dimensions as well. The integral, binding nature of this dimension is perhaps more readily obvious than any of the other dimensions. Without the inspiration of the Holy Spirit as its foundation, the dimensions of the church remain

---

11. Congar, *I Believe in the Holy Spirit*, 167–72.

lifeless and empty, they ossify and deprive the church of its vitality and make inevitable a time of reformation, along with a possible fragmentation, sometime in the future.

The pentecostal dimension can, therefore, be likened to the fuel of the church by which each dimension expresses itself with vitality and effectiveness. It is animated by the Holy Spirit proceeding from the divine source, which provides grace for the healing and restoration of a sinful people seeking to live in communion with God and one another in love. The church finds her ground in God by remaining in the Spirit. She maintains her indefectible self through the power of this same Spirit. She gathers the world community into her embrace through this very same Spirit.

As the animating force for the life of the church, the Spirit enlivens the human spirit and the various gifts given to each for the encouragement and maturation of the people of God. The goal of the Spirit is participation in the Triune life of God through the glorification of the human person made in God's image and likeness. This image and likeness becomes realized through this Spirit who has done the work of purification and sanctification in the human heart. The result is the realization of the kingdom of God in the church now manifest in the various fruits of the Spirit, most preeminently in love.

History has given us ample moments of both repression and release of the pentecostal dimension as our brief survey has demonstrated. The birth of the church was most fundamentally a pentecostal experience and the Spirit remains the dominant presence throughout the early years of the apostolic age. For the early Christians, the Spirit was the Spirit of Christ who had not died and ascended to God the Father to remain there in heaven but was in and among them as the one who had triumphed over sin and death. In one single experience of the divine, the Spirit communicated both the transcendent holiness of the divine majesty and the imminent concern of the divine Friend. Human and divine are made one through this Spirit.

This integral polarity has proven very difficult to maintain and balance. The tendency through the years has been either toward neglect or extremism. Ever since St. Paul in Corinth, pastorally guiding the church between the extremes of enthusiasm and formalism has been fraught with ambiguity and heartache much to the detriment of the wholeness of the church. One thing has become obvious in recent years, however: the Spirit in our day and age is a force with which we must contend and find new ways to integrate into the overall ecclesial shape of the church. It seems, thankfully, that neglect is becoming less and less an option. A more pressing challenge, though, is the various enthusiastic movements which have formed niche communities content to exist apart from dimensions integral to the overall catholicity of the church. The pentecostal dimension, while crucial to the wellbeing of the church and foundational to the life of the church, is still one dimension among others that functions properly only when integrated with the whole. Going rogue, the pentecostal dimension tends toward emotional excess and fantastical delusions. Without the evangelical dimension, it is without content and focus and preaches experience for experience's sake. Without the discipline of the intellectual dimension, it becomes saccharine sentimentality vulnerable to charismatic, manipulative leaders. Without the mystical dimension, it is content to remain on the surface of undependable and unpredictable feelings. Without the sacramental and liturgical dimension, it drifts toward chaos struggling to find appropriate expressions in which to incarnate itself. Without the pastoral dimension, it can easily turn in on itself becoming preoccupied with the next "experience of God" and on its own power. Without the prophetic dimension, it becomes satisfied with its own accomplishments of kingdom fulfillment and sacrifices the poor and marginalized at the altar of spiritual gluttony.

But with the pentecostal dimension the church can proclaim the Word of God with inspiration and conviction and bear witness to the kingdom of God with humility and grace. It can bring spiritual insight and wisdom to the searching mind. It guides and protects the church in the contemplation of the divine reality and not just on natural and profane ones. It directs the church to experience the sacraments and liturgy in an authentic encounter and inspires true worship instead of a dry, repetitive formalism. It makes the pastoral office a joy in its service instead of just another job that breeds resentment for its costly demands. It puts the church in touch with the heart of God for those whose dignity has been assaulted and inspires heroic, selfless action on their behalf instead of relying on empty platitudes.

In my initial thoughts about the pentecostal dimension, I had conceived of this dimension as the "charismatic" dimension. This, I ultimately considered, a temptation to be avoided. A problem I see that is currently preventing the church from enjoying her integral fullness is allowing the pentecostal dimension to be co-opted into a truncated version of itself. Understanding the Spirit in the church merely through its charismatic lens, particularly through its most contemporary iteration of it, is an all too myopic vision for the full role the Spirit has to play to make the church all that it is called to be. Words matter, especially in this case. By overemphasizing charismatic gifts and empowerment, the church is in danger of sidestepping one of the Spirit's integral functions, which is to make holy and transform the human heart into the heart of Christ. The ugly side of this defect in approach can be seen in the gross, self-serving lives of many disgraced televangelists and their perverted prosperity gospel. Pentecost can never be proclaimed apart from the cross. If we go that route, we're left with only hype and are set firmly on the path of emotional manipulation and enthusiasm. An integral approach saves us from such a misguided venture and gets us back on the straight and narrow.

CHAPTER 3

The Church at Worship in a Symbolic World

The Sacramental Dimension

SCRIPTURAL ROOTS

One of the foundational presuppositions of the sacramental dimension of the church is that the term *sacramental* is meant to be broadly interpreted and is in no way meant to be limited to the official sacraments of the church (whether seven or two or any other number). Within this broad approach to sacramentality, both the inherent sacredness of creation and the liturgical aspects of the church will come to the fore.

The sacramentality of the church is fully grounded in the sacramentality of Israel as the people of God which, in turn, is grounded in the sacramentality of the world as God's good creation. Even after sin enters the world, creation remains the conduit through which God encounters humankind made in the divine image. Each theophanic encounter recorded in the pages of the Old Testament demonstrates the use of matter to mediate the divine presence and communicate the divine will, each resulting in human transformation and the realization of the divine purpose in the world through the reception of God's empowering presence received in the encounter. Often, these theophanic encounters lead either directly or eventually to some form of liturgical response where worship and thanksgiving are offered to God for God's graciousness. For Israel, this often meant the utilization of matter in the form of sacrificial offering. The order of creation, then, becomes the normative manner in which God touches humankind and transforms it and the way humankind seeks to touch God in return and forge into a deeper bond the relationship between human and divine.

Moses, as the chosen mediator between God and Israel, encounters God in the fire of the burning bush. The divine voice is heard, the divine will is made known, and the divine presence empowers Moses to fulfill the commission to which he is sent. Immediately before the exodus event, God instructs Moses and Aaron about the celebration of the Passover and its annual celebration as a memorial of God's saving fidelity to Israel. Immediately after the exodus event, Israel breaks into songs of praise in worship of her saving God.

The other sacramental instruments of God's saving presence in the Hebrew Bible are numerous: Noah's Ark and the flood waters; the rite of circumcision; Abraham's theophanic encounter at Mamre; Moses' staff; the tablets of stone; the tabernacle and its contents; the priesthood and priestly garments and rituals; the sacred calendar and festivals; the ark of the covenant, just to name some from the Pentateuch alone.

The temple in Jerusalem would become the pinnacle of divine/human encounter for the people of Israel and the locus of Israelite sacramentality. Painstaking detail was carefully related in the construction of the elements of the Temple in order to imbue each element with sacred meaning and foster the divine/human encounter. The result of worship in the Temple was the sanctification of the people of Israel who worshiped there and the guarantee of their blessing and prosperity. Put more succinctly, the purpose of every Israelite was the glorification of Yahweh, whose loving fidelity was proven constantly throughout Israel's history. This glorification took place in two primary, yet, integrally related, ways: through Israel's cultic acts of worship and her life of obedience to Torah. Both, the prophets would often have to insist, are to issue from a heart that has been won over by Yahweh's loving fidelity and not simply from ritual obligation or fear of retribution.

Even after the destruction of the Temple, the people of Israel would continue to seek ways of maintaining the divine/human relationship, now primarily through their life of fidelity to Torah expressed through gathering together in synagogues, listening to the sacred story of Israel's salvation history, and celebrating the sacred festivals of that history in her own day, thus concretizing God's saving events for herself in her own time. Thus, while the form that her gathered worship took changed over the various periods of her life according to the circumstances in which she found herself, never was there a time in Israel's history when she was non-liturgical. Israel's prophets, rather than being anti-ritualists, functioned to assure Israel's liturgical authenticity from the heart.

The symbolic world of Israel was thus a full immersion in cultic sacramentality which found its basis on the good creation formed by the hand of Yahweh. As co-creators made in the image and likeness of God, the people of Israel stood apart as the chosen people to receive the particular revelation through which God would manifest the divine Name and Presence. This manifestation was always and everywhere mediated through Israel's particular symbolic world. The divine Presence manifested and encountered was always considered the privileged goal of Israelite life and worship and was what allowed Israel to receive the grace to remain faithful to the covenantal bond that her god initiated with her. In his opening paragraph to his chapter on Israel's cultic life, Walter Breuggemann, in his *Theology of the Old Testament: Testimony, Dispute, Advocacy*, writes,

> The textual traditions concerning Israel's worship are rich and diverse. They are agreed, however, in their primary claim that the cult, in its many forms and expressions, mediates Yahweh's "real presence." In worship, Israel is dealing with the person, character, will, purpose, and presence of Yahweh. While this presence is *mediated* by ritual and sacramental practice, it is the *real presence* of Yahweh that is mediated. Thus these texts about worship seek to articulate and make available real presence. More than that, the concrete practice of these rituals and sacraments shaped Israel as a community related intensely and definitionally to Yahweh.[1]

The divine/human encounter reaches its apogee in the incarnation of the Son of God and creates new opportunities for the people of God to encounter the divine in the symbolic, sacramental world in which they live. In continuity with the Israelite sacramental and liturgical life on which their Christian life was based, the early followers of Jesus of Nazareth began to reimagine their sacramental and liturgical world in light of the teachings and witness of Jesus, most significantly, in light of his death and resurrection and the experience of his Spirit poured out upon them on the day of Pentecost. For them, the presence of God was now made available in an unprecedented way and access to God became unrestricted. For them, also, the divine/human relationship was now open to potentially greater depths than ever before, since, those recreated anew in Christ are made sharers of the divine nature and are now being transformed from glory to glory. The

---

1. Brueggemann, *Theology of the Old Testament: Testimony, Dispute, Advocacy*, 650.

divine *Presence*, then, as it was for Israel, was also the central theme of the early Christians' understanding of the unique offer made to the world in Christ Jesus.

What was in slight discontinuity, however, was the shape that the sacramental and liturgical life of the early Christians would take. Christian Baptism and the Lord's Supper or Eucharist would become the two central sacramental experiences which would initiate the Christian into Christ and would, in turn, inform the way Christians would experience God (and Christ) in their worship. This experience unlocked, for Christians, the hidden potential in creation now made explicit in the Incarnation. Now, more than ever before, creation mediates the divine presence and accomplishes its divinely sanctioned end of being an instrument in the wedding of human and divine.

The sacramental dimension of the church is, therefore, based upon a sacramental vision which sees Baptism and Eucharist as the fullest expression of the sacramental potential of creation where two primary ends are achieved: the *sanctification* of the people of God with its concomitant offering of worship to God in the liturgy and the *formation of community.*

For St. Paul, in the sacrament of Baptism the Christian is made a new creation and a child of God in a unique and definitive way. The old self is put off and the new self is liberated to live unimpeded by the old pattern of sin and death. All Christians together are baptized into the one body of Christ and are, thereby, members of one another living and working in unity of Spirit in order to gather all of creation into Christ. In the Eucharist, heaven and earth become one in one unified act of praise and thanksgiving as all Christians together partake of the one bread and one cup of the body and blood of Christ. The church is, thus, not only initiated into Christ in the Eucharist but is also continually nurtured on this bread from heaven, the mercy and grace of God that is more than sufficient for the church's journey to the final restoration of all things in Christ.

The liturgical expression of the church in worship is, thus, a constitutive element of the sacramental dimension of the church. Although justly emphasizing the sacramental rites of Baptism and Eucharist, the liturgy of the church is far more encompassing. It has come to include other sacramental rites (many already intimated in the New Testament) such as anointings with oil (for healing, confirmation, and ordination), marriage, and reconciliation. It includes gestures in worship and prayers that unify and express the church's common desire to bless and be blessed by God. It seeks to sanctify time by remembering and bringing into the present the sacred events of the Lord's life, death, resurrection, and ascension, along with the bestowal of his Spirit, which form the liturgical seasons. It celebrates the communion of saints and helps the church to become aware of and benefit from their ongoing presence in the one body of Christ. It utilizes the arts to offer fitting praise and thanksgiving to God and thus gives emphasis to music and image, architecture and furnishings. It engages the senses with incense and light, icons and stained-glass windows. The sacred object becomes not an idol that diverts from God but a window into eternity where God is made more explicitly known. In turn, the church's liturgy, while serving to awaken our vision of God in heaven, perhaps, more importantly, awakens our vision of God in the world where we remain. Sacramental initiation into God enlivens the inner senses to begin to apprehend God hidden, yet, vitally present, in all things. In so doing, the sacramental dimension of the church reorients and orders life according to life's depth dimension and brings it face to face with the mystical dimension. It's no wonder that the sacraments in the Greek east are known as *mysteria*. All of these sacramental developments in the life of the church are firmly rooted in the life of the early Christians attested to in the pages of the New Testament. That there were problems along the pathway of this development during the succeeding generations of Christianity has played no small role in the church's dis*integration*. A rightly understood and biblically based sacramentality will be, then, crucial in reintegrating the church toward a healthy wholeness.

DEFINING CHARACTERISTICS

Although the sacramental dimension of the church underwent great development through the centuries, and continues to do so, several important points should be made in light of our biblical survey which highlight the fundamental roots of this dimension.

- *Creation,* as an act of God, *is fundamentally good* and retains its ability to convey the divine even after sin enters the world.
- *The presence of God* throughout the Hebrew Bible *is often made manifest through matter.*
- The human encounter with God mediated through matter is *revelatory* of the divine will and divine self and is *transformative* in nature.

- The normative human response to the divine, sacramental encounter in the Hebrew Bible is *worship* and *thanksgiving*.
- The *liturgy is a direct response* to this divine/human encounter.
- Not only is the liturgy of the Israelites a human response to God's divine intervention, it is also presented as *a direct command of God*, often presented in meticulous detail and specificity.
- Even though the worship of Israel forbad any created image of God, a plethora of *symbolic furnishings* and *gestures* were involved.
- The *physical senses*, then, *played a vital role* in the worship of Israel.
- The worship of Israel was most often portrayed in the Hebrew Bible in its *communal form*.
- *The interior disposition of the heart* in Israel's worship came to be of utmost concern, particularly in the ministry of the prophets.
- *The incarnation of the Son of God serves as the theological basis* for understanding the central role sacramentality would take in the life of the church.
- The *Sacraments of Baptism and Eucharist*, both instituted by Jesus himself, would reshape the way the early Christians, who were mostly Jews, would worship and understand their relationship with God.
- Both of these sacraments place emphasis on the *interior disposition* of the one initiated into Christ: Baptism as a *circumcision of the heart* and adoption as a child of God; the Eucharist as a *taking in* (feeding and drinking) *of the divine life* of the Son of God and a *participation* in that divine life.
- Flowing from the gift of the Spirit and entirely dependent upon it, the sacramental dimension of the church *leads toward the deepening of the union between human and divine* and, thus, inevitably nurtures within the initiated the mystical dimension.

The controversy that would envelop the church at various points in its history, whether during the time of the iconoclast dispute or during the Protestant Reformation, is already a struggle in the life of Israel in her dual affirmation of the goodness of creation, with its developing cult of Yahweh, and her insistence that Yahweh can never be cast into an image. The continual threat of idolatry and the experience of the expulsion from the Promised Land due to its idolatrous infidelity, seared within the consciousness of Israel the ongoing threat that idolatrous practice posed, along with the horrors that resulted from it. Yet, one is hard pressed to find anywhere in the pages of the Hebrew Bible where Israel was anything remotely what we might call today non-sacramental. Her cult as well as her spirituality in general were highly mediated forms of being in this world as she related to Yahweh. One could even argue that, in practicality, Judaism has been more at home in the body than Christianity, whose Greek influence has cast a broad shadow over the physical world. Much of Christianity's integration/reintegration of the physical world has, in fact, come through uncovering its Jewish roots. With this has come a new/renewed appreciation of the sacramental dimension of the church based on the sacramentality of all creation.

That the sacramental dimension of the church has exerted itself at times with such enduring and potent force is a testament to its staying power. That it has been sidelined and even excised from parts of the church is a testament to the church's continual struggle with regarding the natural world as revelatory—human nature, in particular. The reality of sin and its pervasiveness is at the heart of this conversation and controversy. But this is only one aspect of what has made the sacramental dimension problematic. The other, and more ancient, is the holiness of God. The question that was posed to the church rather early on was: has the incarnation qualified at all the assertion that God cannot and ought not be depicted in the form of an image? It is with this question that we begin our survey of the sacramental dimension in church history.

THE SACRAMENTAL DIMENSION IN CHURCH HISTORY

The Iconoclast Controversy

Two theological systems came head to head in the Eastern Church from the early eighth century until the middle of the ninth: the strict monotheism of Judaism, with its commandment against the worship of graven images, and the belief in the incarnation in Christianity. Of course, as an inheritor of the monotheistic tradition of Judaism, Christianity would uphold the idea of a single deity. The challenge presented itself in the idea that the Son of God, the second person of this single deity, was made flesh and dwelt among us. The question became: does the incarnation of the Son of

God qualify the stricture against the reverence of images of the divine? This clash of theologies, as mentioned, worked itself out mainly in the Christian East, particularly in the theological responses to the controversy by John of Damascus (d. 773) and Theodore the Studite (d. 826). John of Damascus held that, "[We] do not adore creation; [we] worship the One who assumed creation.... God has saved [us] through matter.... Because of the incarnation, [we] salute all creation."[2] This theological position would be ratified by the Seventh Ecumenical Council in 787 which declared that the use of icons was a "guarantee that the divine incarnation of the Word is real and not illusory."[3]

The spirituality that would receive approbation from this decision is insightfully captured by John Chryssavgis:

> Thus, Christian art became as essential a part of Eastern Christian spiritual life and thought as theology and the sacraments. More than merely incidental, ornamental or even instructional, icons are theology and spirituality in colour. They constitute a channel of divine grace and sanctification. They are a liturgical art, a way of prayer, an article of faith, a fact of immediate experience of a mystery beyond experience. The world of the icon offers new insights and new perceptions into reality, revealing the eternal dimension in the world of sense and experience. Icons signify a sacred covenant, a symbolical connection between our selves and our world, since both humanity and nature are created. Moreover, icons indicate a desire for intimate communion and mutual enhancement between our world and the beyond....
>
> The icon restores and reconciles, reminding of another way and of another world. It offers a corrective to a self-centered or world-centered culture that gives value only to the here and now. The icon aspires to the inner vision of all, the world as created and as intended by God.... The icon does away with any objective distance between this world and the next, between the material and the spiritual, between body and soul, time and eternity, creation and divinity. The icon reminds us that there is no double vision, no double order in creation. The icon speaks in this world the language of the age to come.[4]

Grounding this spirituality is the fundamental capacity of creation and human nature to mediate the divine. Chryssavgis explains that in iconography,

---

2. Quoted in Chryssavgis, "Iconography," 353.
3. Quoted in Chryssavgis, "Iconography," 353.
4. Chryssavgis, "Iconography," 353.

"the human person exists on two levels and worlds simultaneously. The human person is considered a meeting point for all of creation, a bridge between this world and heaven."[5] For Theodore the Studite, "The fact that the human person is created in the image and likeness of God means that the making of icons is in some way a divine work."[6] For Irenaeus of Lyons, as early as the second century, the capacity for mediation goes far beyond human nature: "everything is a sign of God."[7]

The Radical Reformation

Much had changed in the church and the context was significantly different for the church at the time of the Protestant Reformation in the West. Not satisfied with the efforts of reform coming from Luther, Calvin, and Zwingli, those advocating for a more radical reformation advocated for a more thoroughgoing stripping away of the perceived accretions to the life of the church that were deemed distortions to the primitive way of Christianity enjoyed by the first disciples. A characteristic impulse of this movement was an iconoclastic disgust against images that not only were deemed a distraction from a transcendent God but, more grievously, a participation in the sin of idolatry. Other points of emphasis were understanding the sacraments as attestations of the faith already active, mere *ordinances* which do not mediate grace in and of themselves; a divesting of any theological jargon or ecclesial practice that did not have clearly expressed articulation in the Bible; a curtailment of tradition as a valid rule of faith; an extreme skepticism of the world as offering any positive contribution to the life of the church.

The primary concern of the movements which make up the Radical Reformation was the preservation of a living faith which authentically attests to a life of Christian discipleship. Anything that threatened this living faith was discarded and, most often, despised. The sacramentalism of the time posed, for them, a serious pastoral and spiritual problem: one can be deceived in thinking that just because they have received the sacraments, in the case of Infant Baptism even before the possibility of active faith, that they are Christians regardless of whether their life attests to this faith through their actions. The leaders of these movements saw something even

---

5. Chryssavgis, "Iconography," 354.
6. Quoted in Chryssavgis, "Iconography," 354.
7. Quoted in Chryssavgis, "Iconography," 354.

more pernicious at work: while the sacraments were meant to initiate and nurture the Christian in one's faith they already have, in effect, they become the very stumbling block on which authentic faith has fallen and lost its saving power. This, they critique, has led to a church full of nominal Christians sacramentalized without being truly transformed from within, left deluded that they are what in fact they are not. Such a serious critique required an equally serious response and no compromise could be tolerated. This primal revulsion to this theological, spiritual, and pastoral problem led to a hyper focus on understanding faith purely as a subjective reality within the life of the Christian and a hyper skepticism to any external, material, or formal action that inherently expresses or nurtures faith. No external aspect of Christian faith could be allowed to mask the authentic faith issuing forth from the believer's heart.

These understandably valid concerns were nothing new to the life of the church. Many other ecclesial movements had already had similar concerns and many would for centuries to come after the sixteenth century. One notable movement that predated the Protestant Reformation by some four-hundred years was the Cistercian reform. The impulses of the early reformers of this monastic movement originating in Citeaux, France have striking similarities to the impulses of the radical reformers. The Cistercian reform is characterized by a concern for authentic faith, inner transformation, and a skepticism of images that were deemed to be distractions to a transcendent God. Yet, their impulses did not lead to the radical iconoclasm and skepticism of the material world, sacraments, or liturgy that characterized the Protestant radicals. The both/and approach that characterized the larger tradition of Christianity was maintained, although emphasis was quite intentionally placed on the inner life. The various elements of Christian life were, in a way, renegotiated and reappropriated and reintegrated in a way that gave proper emphasis to each. The either/or approach of the Protestant radical reformers was more intolerable to such nuance. The world in which they inhabited was no longer a possible reflection of the divine glory extending grace and transcendence but a trap and temptation to guard against and from which to protect oneself. The world as symbolic and inviting would, most especially in these ecclesial movements, begin its descent and demise. The valid concerns for a living faith would in the end through its isolationism truncate and deprive this same faith's nourishment and growth.

THE SHAPE OF THE CHURCH

The English Reformation and the Oxford Movement

The two literary products of the English Reformation, *The Book of Common Prayer* of 1549 and the Authorized Version of the Bible (King James Version), attests to the inherent convictions embedded in the minds of these reformers. The Church of England was to be built upon the two pillars of the liturgy (prayer in community and its common worship) and the Word of God. It was to remain a sacramental and liturgical church who now gave proper place and value to the gospel revealed in Sacred Scripture. In opposition to the growing push among some who were dissatisfied with the extent of the reform (who came to be called Puritans), the newly established church would stand its ground and hold on to what was deemed beneficial and integral to ecclesial life. On the other end, it would also have to wrestle with the push to move back to the fold of Roman Catholicism and forgo the convictions that fueled the reform. After many years of this tug of war back and forth, what resulted was a unique expression of the Christian church that has been widely recognized as a *via media*. By nature, then, Anglicanism is constituted toward integration and balance. This, of course, does not mean it is in fact the most integrated or balanced among the various ecclesial bodies of Christianity. What it does mean is that it, particularly when it comes to the sacramental and evangelical dimensions, is quite intentionally a both/and communion, and, perhaps, offers the wider church a paradigm toward greater wholeness.

Anglicanism, today, has the capacity to hold within its fold a wide diversity of ecclesial expressions. Not all movements that it has generated have remained within its fold but many have. The most notable break was among the evangelical Methodist movement in the years following the deaths of John and Charles Wesley, its brother founders. Nevertheless, a great many Anglicans today would wholeheartedly embrace their evangelical heritage. On the Catholic side of the Anglican spectrum, the movement that has asserted itself most pervasively within Anglicanism is no doubt the Oxford Movement of the nineteenth century.

Led by a small group of professors of Oxford University, most notably John Keble (1792–1866), John Henry Newman (1801–1890), and Edward Bouverie Pusey (1800–1882), this movement within The Church of England would advocate, through its primary series of publications, *The Tracts for the Times*, for what characterized its High Church heritage in continuity with the Caroline Divines of the seventeenth century. These "Tractarians" argued for the authority of an ordained ministry stemming from apostolic times along the lines of an unbroken apostolic succession and for the renewal of sacramental theology with particular emphasis given to what was deemed the real presence of Christ in the Eucharist. They also argued for an understanding of evangelical conversion that moved away from Protestant theories of justification. Newman's momentous departure from Anglicanism into Roman Catholicism proved to be a severe blow to the movement's credibility, but under the leadership of Keble and Pusey, Anglo-Catholicism, as it came to be called, would grow and establish itself throughout worldwide Anglicanism. Potential for building ecumenical relations among various ecclesial communities has been a high priority for Anglicans, both inspiring the modern ecumenical movement and being one of its most ardent voices. Its unique embrace of both sacramental and evangelical dimensions which constitute its heritage and ecclesial identity have given to Anglicanism this natural proclivity toward inclusion.

The Liturgical Movement

The modern Liturgical Movement refers to the efforts which the Roman Catholic Church made during the nineteenth century leading up to the Second Vatican Council in moving the liturgy from what was largely a private matter performed by clergy to its proper role as one that promotes the active participation of all believers. Pastoral concerns were, thus, at the heart of this movement. What resulted, in the end, was the implementation of many of the issues that concerned the Protestant reformers of the sixteenth century but which Trent was too reluctant to adopt. The Roman Catholic Church was now, having become rather far removed from the polemically charged atmosphere of the sixteenth century, ready for change.

The original inspiration for the modern Liturgical Movement is to be found at the Abbey of Solesme whose founder, Dom Prosper Guéranger (1805–1875), was the intellectual and spiritual force behind the movement. Following the intellectual awakening of the Age of Enlightenment, it was the desire of many of the leaders of the nineteenth century to connect themselves with the great Tradition of the church. This opened up unforeseen opportunities well beyond liturgical practice and would affect the church in all its dimensions. This is especially true, however, for the sacramental/liturgical dimension. A greater understanding of the original context and meaning of the events of Scripture as well as the Apostolic Fathers and those to follow in the Patristic era challenged certain theological presuppositions and practices about the liturgy. Liturgical developments were now able to be criticized according to the Tradition. Going back to the sources meant going back to a more authentic and sound belief and practice. Particularly, for Guéranger, this meant the restoration of Benedictine life in France whose liturgy, now grounded in a theology free from the accretions and aberrations of centuries far removed from the Patristic era and in a revitalized Gregorian chant, imbued the worship experience with both greater theological clarity and sense and a corresponding aesthetic and sacramental expression. This wedding of intellect and liturgical embodiment would do much to lay the foundations for a more integral relationship between theology and worship in the years to come.

At the beginning of the twentieth century, the movement would gain traction through the efforts of Dom Lambert Beauduin (1873–1960) and his community of Mont César in Louvain, Belgium. Having worked as a diocesan priest and chaplain for several years and inspired by Leo XIII's social encyclical *Rerum Novarum* of 1891, Beauduin, now a monk of Mont César, would promote liturgical action which envisaged the spread of this renewed sense of liturgical life that would include all peoples of society into its fold, not just an intellectual or clerical elite. Beauduin also challenged the individual spiritualities that had become so popular during this period and argued that the liturgy was an authentic religious experience that was vital, not only to personal faith, but to the life of the church as a whole. More than that, it opened up new encounters with God that can only be experienced in community and as community and demonstrated, in doing so, that personal faith development is severely handicapped without this communal dimension.

Beauduin's efforts would be quite effective in helping the movement spread throughout the Roman Catholic world and would inspire Dom Virgil Michel (1890–1938) of St. John's Abbey in Collegeville, Minnesota to become the catalyst for the dissemination of the movement in the United States. Notable is the emphasis that the Liturgical Movement, both here in the US and, before it arrived here, in Europe, placed on social issues. This certainly was influenced by the context of the historical period of the movement at this point which was the post-depression era, but it also was undoubtedly intentional and is grounded in a liturgical theology rooted in the Christ who came to feed the hungry, heal the sick, and comfort the dying. This commitment to wedding liturgy with social action parallels directly with the concerns of the Oxford Movement in Anglicanism that immediately preceded the modern Liturgical Movement in Roman Catholicism.

With the Second Vatican Council's Constitution on the Liturgy *Sacrosanctum Concilium*, the Roman Catholic Church would thoroughly reform its liturgical life based upon the work done by so many over the course of the previous century. The presider now faced the congregation, the congregation now prayed and worshiped in the vernacular, communion was received in both bread and wine, the Divine Office was promoted as a form of prayer for all, the revised lectionary exposed the faithful to a much broader selection of Sacred Scripture, preaching was now given much greater emphasis, and The Rite of Christian Initiation of Adults (RCIA) was formed to more adequately guide newcomers into a fuller, more thoughtful, embrace of their life as Roman Catholic Christians. All of this would quite radically change the face of modern Catholicism but would also lead to the liturgical wars within the communion that now characterize the contemporary Roman Catholic Church.

The modern Liturgical Movement would, however, exert great influence beyond the bounds of the Roman Catholic Church. All liturgical churches, especially in the West, have been influenced by the insights generated by this movement, and the movement has served as a potent ecumenical force in the modern church.

Rahner and Schillebeeckx

Particular points of emphasis in sacramental theology began to be made during the modern period which served to move the understanding of the sacraments from a more myopic vision which focused on the quantity (how many sacraments?), the nature (substance and accidents), and effect (sacramental grace) to a wider understanding which considered the topics of personal encounter, ecclesiology, and worship. This shift in focus is reflected is reflected in Vatican Council II's *Constitution on the Sacred Liturgy* when it says,

> The purpose of the Sacraments is to sanctify participants, to build up the body of Christ, and, finally to give worship to God; because they are signs they also instruct. They not only presuppose faith, but by words and objects they also nourish, strengthen, and express it; that is why they are called 'Sacraments of faith.' They do indeed impart grace, but, in addition, the very act of celebrating

them most effectively disposes the faithful to receive this grace in a fruitful manner, to worship God duly, and to practice charity.[8]

Two primary theological minds lie behind this new direction in the understanding of the Sacraments in the Roman Catholic Church. Karl Rahner (1904-1984) and Edward Schillebeeckx (1914-2009), both working out their ecclesiology and sacramental theology during the same pre-conciliar period, attempted to understand the sacraments with more comprehensive definitions in terms of Christ and the church. For Rahner, the church is the sacrament of God's saving activity in the world. It is "the historically real and actual presence of the eschatologically victorious mercy of God," and "the sign of the grace of God definitely triumphant in the world in Christ."[9] Against the criticism that Roman Catholicism has tended to reduce the Kingdom of God to the church, Rahner clarifies that the church "is the sacrament of the Kingdom of God in the eschatological phase of sacred history which began with Christ, the phase which brings about the kingdom of God."[10] From the infinite horizon of God's eternal presence, God has, for Rahner, in Christ, become not only definitively available but actually present and invites creation to enter into this transforming presence to participate in God's own life. This participation is at once in Spirit and in sacrament. It is the sanctification and participation of the total person in both its physical and spiritual dimensions; hence it is both in Spirit and in sacrament.

For Schillebeeckx, the shift in the Roman Catholic understanding of the sacraments occurred primarily because of its own self-understanding of what it means to be church. Its sacramental theology is rooted and determined by its ecclesiology. Schillebeeckx saw and did much to promote the understanding of the church as the *sacramentum mundi* ("sacrament of the world"). *World*, in this context, refers to the community of human beings in fellowship and dialogue with one another. The church bears the responsibility of dialoguing with the world along its journey in history toward greater human fulfillment and offers to the world the full realization of human possibility. So he can say, "The Church's critical function is not that of an outsider, pursuing a parallel path, but rather that of one who

---

8. *Sacrosanctum Concilium*, 59.

9. Rahner, *The Church and the Sacraments*, pp. 14 and 18, cited in McBrien, *Catholicism*, 692.

10. Rahner, "Church and World" in *The Concise Sacramentum Mundi*, 239, cited in McBrien, *Catholicism*, 692.

is critically involved in the building of the world and the progress of the nations."[11] The sacramental presence of the church is far from a static ideal removed from the concerns of real people. It is the dynamic inbreaking of the Kingdom of God extending the hand of God . . . touching, blessing, healing, and saving.

Schillebeeckx's primary work in sacramental theology was his influential text of 1963, *Christ the Sacrament of the Encounter with God*. In it, far from repudiating his scholastic forebears, he quite intentionally makes connections with them, particularly with his Dominican confrere, Thomas Aquinas. As one reviewer noted, "seldom has Thomas Aquinas looked so good."[12] Central to Schillebeeckx's thesis is the idea of encounter. A gap between God and humankind is presupposed and serves as the fundamental problem facing the human predicament. This is not solely a result of sin but also a condition of human finiteness. In order to bridge the gap, God initiates an encounter with humankind whose definitive basis is found in the incarnation. In Christ is the encounter of divine and human. For Schillebeeckx, this encounter is extended in time in the sacramental life of the church where God continues the work of encounter and of bridging the gap. Past, present, and future converge precisely in the sacraments through *anamnesis* (the commemoration of Christ's saving events), through the present sacramental action and bestowal of grace, and through the inbreaking of the eschatological fullness of the glorified Christ encountered in the sacramental presence.

What has resulted from the work of these two formidable theologians who did so much to shape *Sacrosanctum concilium* and the post-conciliar church is an imbuing of the sacramental life of the church with a spiritual vitality and breadth it had struggled for years to develop. Instead of choosing the route of sacramental marginalization, the route chosen by the radical reformers, the renewal of sacramental theology and the liturgy along with it that characterized twentieth-century Roman Catholicism, and through it other sacramental ecclesial communities, chose the route of integrating the tradition with other then current philosophical and theological disciplines which infused the tradition with new life and relevance. It was precisely this integral approach that unlocked hidden potentials with traditional sacramental theology and placed the sacraments, and, with it, a sacramental worldview, front and center in the life of the church. So much so, that

---

11. Schillebeeckx, *God the Future of Man*, 161, cited in McBrien, *Catholicism*, 694.
12. Bertram, Review of *Christ the Sacrament of the Encounter with God*.

non-sacramental ecclesial communities in recent years are taking notice and beginning to reevaluate their tendency of sacramental marginalization.

Sacramentality and Its Resurgence in the Contemporary Church

The broadening trend in situating discussion on the official sacraments of the church in the more general seedbed of the sacramentality of the church, and in the primal sacrament of Christ, has led sacramental theologians to insist more strongly than ever before in keeping all of these dimensions of sacramental theology together. Kevin W. Irwin, in his article "A Sacramental World–Sacramentality As The Primary Language for Sacraments," draws attention to this multidimensional relationship when he states: "We live in a sacramental world and it is through the liturgy's use of the things of this world that we experience particularly 'strong moments' of God's self-disclosure."[13] He continues,

> In a sacramental world view the world in which we live is interdependent – all that dwell in it are part of God's plan for us all. It is also a locus where God is revealed, disclosed and experienced. This means the world, humans and all creatures great and small, are all signs of God among us. It also means taking seriously 'daily and domestic things,' for these are the tangible ways and means the church uses to experience and partake in the life of God both in liturgy and sacraments and outside of them in all of life . . . . My premise is that 'sacramentality' comes first; rituals of liturgy and sacraments derive from it. Then they return us to this graced world. The celebrations of liturgy and sacraments are integral to and integrating of the Christian life lived in a sacramental world.[14]

The integralism embedded in the sacramental worldview, for Irwin, coincides with what he calls the "rhetoric of sacramentality" that is always "both . . . and" rather than "either . . . or." A sacramental worldview acknowledges that the world is simultaneously both graced and in need of final redemption. In light of this presupposition, Irwin draws the juxtaposition thus: "In an 'either . . . or' framework sacraments offer escapes from the world and send us back to it charged to work more adequately in it for the cause of

---

13. Irwin, "A Sacramental World–Sacramentality As The Primary Language for Sacraments."

14. Irwin, "A Sacramental World–Sacramentality As The Primary Language for Sacraments."

God's kingdom. In a sacramental world, it is the world itself that is, in the words of Gerard Manley Hopkins, 'charged with the grandeur of / God . . . ./ Because the Holy Ghost over the bent/ World broods with warm breast and with / ah! Bright wings.'"[15]

Irwin concludes his article by emphasizing the integral nature of the sacramental worldview for which he argues throughout his article by drawing a final, resulting implication. For him, life issuing forth from the renewed sacramental liturgy grounded in a renewed sacramental worldview means that "we live in a sacramental world that is interdependent in terms of persons, things, symbols (and their manufacture) as well as a sacramental premise that sees and finds God in the world. 'Sacramentality' thus implies integration and experiencing God here and now in all of life as well as in what is yet to be in eternity."[16] The liturgy that celebrates with deep and strong ritual expressions is based on the reality of God's abiding presence before, during, and after the sacramental moment. Irwin challenges the way the church has often marginalized the world and dismissed it, referring to it only as the object of what the liturgy leads toward: the world's sanctification. As a corrective to this non-integral approach, he insists that

> [T]he function of sacramental liturgy is less to bring to the world what we have experienced in the liturgy (as important as that truly is) than it is to underscore how what we do in liturgy derives from the world and from everyday life, the liturgical ritualization of which helps us order our lives and our world once more in God's image and likeness. Sacraments are less doors to the sacred than they are the experience of the sacred in human life.[17]

This opening up and expansion of sacramental theology from sacraments to sacramentality has peaked the interest of Protestant communities suspicious of the perceived constrictions and liabilities of the medieval paradigm of sacramental theology and is now causing many of these communities to reevaluate their relationship to the notion of sacramentality and the spiritual benefits derived from it—and is helping some reintegrate

---

15. Irwin, "A Sacramental World–Sacramentality As The Primary Language for Sacraments."

16. Irwin, "A Sacramental World–Sacramentality As The Primary Language for Sacraments."

17. Irwin, "A Sacramental World–Sacramentality As The Primary Language for Sacraments."

sacramental ritual practice into their community worship experiences. Along with this, the notion of sacramentality has also opened up avenues of correspondence with contemporary culture and now offers to the church further opportunities for the reinvention of its sacramental spirituality.

John Drane highlights the fundamental problems of contemporary culture to which sacramentality can speak and help heal. The pace, stridency, and chaotic obsession with efficiency that characterizes most societies in the modern world has failed to produce the quality of life that was promised. A fast food nation, what Drane refers to as a 'McDonaldized' system, has only played into the illusion of personal fulfillment and now perpetuates, especially through technology, greater isolation, frustration, and meaninglessness. Drane notes that "the inherited Western paradigm is widely regarded as fractured and disconnected, highlighting the need for holistic ways of being that can deal with personal fragmentation as well as larger cosmic, cultural and even scientific understandings."[18]

A resulting effect of this societal malaise is the frantic search for meaning apart from institutional forms of organized religious systems (along with their sacraments and rituals). New ways of searching for sacramental meaning have resulted. Drane identifies a few: "aromatherapy (a form of chrism?), psychotherapy (confession?), rebirthing (baptism?), or any number of other 'alternative' therapies . . . ."[19] He notes that "one of the most accessible expressions of popular sacramentality is in club culture and pop music."[20] I might add the sports arena. What all these experiences seek to create and provide is a concrete, tangible, and communal experience of transcendence that takes us beyond our mundane existence and into a quality of life full of meaning and hope. That all these "secular sacraments" are doomed to lead the human person to frustration is attested by the contradiction of the term "secular sacrament." The transcendence to which the human person is constituted is, by nature, beyond the secular. Only the sacred can constitute something sacramental and truly mediate that for which the human heart and spirit desire and need.

Writing in his blog from a post entitled, "The Exciting Future of Evangelical Sacramentalism," Joshua Penduck, an Anglican priest, shows how

18. Drane, "Contemporary Culture and the Reinvention of Sacramental Spirituality," 43.

19. Drane, "Contemporary Culture and the Reinvention of Sacramental Spirituality," 44.

20. Drane, "Contemporary Culture and the Reinvention of Sacramental Spirituality," 44.

notable contemporary evangelicals are being influenced by the theological tradition within Roman Catholicism which did much to influence the outcomes of the Second Vatican Council, namely, the Nouvelle Théologie, with its emphasis on *ressourcement*—a return to the sources in order to allow the tradition to inform contemporary theology. The regrounding in Plato, he notes, opened up these theologians (i.e. Henri de Lubac, most notably) toward a "sacramental ontology," where the universe is more directly correlated to the "being" of God. Penduck explains, "The existence of the universe is dependent and derivative on God. Only God has 'being' completely in himself and from himself. This means that when I say that the universe exists or has 'being', its being is merely participating in the being of God. Its being is like a sign to God's being. Not simply a sign that points the way (like a road sign), but more like a sign that embodies that which it points to."[21] Taking a queue from Henri de Lubac, Penduck states the point succinctly, "Nature 'participates' in the *super*natural simply by existing . . . ."[22] Penduck highlights the theological work of the evangelical Hans Boersma who advocates for a type of "Evangelical *Ressourcement*." For Boersma, evangelicals need not return to Roman Catholicism but should recover aspects of this tradition which can enrich their own tradition and ground it in a more fertile theological soil. Such an evangelical *Ressourcement* would include reading Scripture more theologically and spiritually rather than exclusively through an exegesis lens. In doing so, it would reclaim the sacramental nature of the sacred text, the *sacra pagina*. It would allow the sacraments of Baptism and Eucharist to assert their proper influence and vitality within the life of the church instead of being marginalized to the realm of "ordinance." It would place greater emphasis on liturgy and ecclesiology and could possibly, Penduck suggests, renew evangelicalism much like it renewed Roman Catholicism in the twentieth century; and before that, how the high church sacramentalism of the Caroline Divines helped renew the Church of England in the seventeenth century and the Oxford Movement in the nineteenth century. So too, may a new *ressourecement* help renew the evangelicalism of the twenty-first century.[23]

While evangelicals have long swayed those from sacramental traditions into their fold, and continue to do so, recent years have seen a trend in the opposite direction as well. In a revealing article published in 2019 in

---

21. Penduck, "The Exciting Future of Evangelical Sacramentalism."
22. Penduck, "The Exciting Future of Evangelical Sacramentalism."
23. Penduck, "The Exciting Future of Evangelical Sacramentalism."

America magazine, "Why Evangelical Megachurches are Embracing (Some) Catholic Traditions," Anna Keating drew attention to the changing tide happening in her hometown of Colorado Springs, a long-time bastion of evangelicalism and home of the ten-thousand member nondenominational New Life Church. Current trends at New Life now include the recitation of the Nicene Creed, the celebration of the Lord's Supper on most Sundays, and teachings on the liturgical calendar. The pastor can be seen wearing a stole with the image of Our Lady of Guadalupe blazoned on it.[24]

The Village Church, a Southern-Baptist megachurch in Flower Mound, TX, boasting over fourteen-thousand members, now observes the liturgical calendar, recites the Apostles' Creed and fasts during Lent.[25] Similar movements are happening at other notable megachurches throughout the country: Willow Creek in Chicago; Mars Hill in Grand Rapids, MI; Epiphany Church in the Dallas/ForthWorth metroplex.[26] Keating notes that in her hometown of Colorado Springs, eighty percent of the congregation at Holy Theophany Orthodox Church are converts from evangelical and Protestant backgrounds.[27] The most common testimony given by these converts highlights the fullness of their Christian faith now experienced through their participation in a more robust sacramental and liturgical life.

TOWARD AN INTEGRAL SACRAMENTAL ECCLESIAL SHAPE

The integral nature of the sacramental dimension of the church is brought out to the fore by Alexander Schmemann, the notable Orthodox liturgical theologian, who writes, "the liturgy of the Word is as sacramental as the sacrament is 'evangelical.'"[28] He continues, "The sacrament is a manifestation of the Word. And unless the false dichotomy between Word and sacrament is overcome, the true meaning of Christian 'sacramentalism' cannot

---

24. Keating, "Why Evangelical Megachurches are Embracing (Some) Catholic Traditions."

25. Keating, "Why Evangelical Megachurches are Embracing (Some) Catholic Traditions."

26. Keating, "Why Evangelical Megachurches are Embracing (Some) Catholic Traditions."

27. Keating, "Why Evangelical Megachurches are Embracing (Some) Catholic Traditions."

28. Schmemann, *For the Life of the World*, 32–33.

be grasped in all their wonderful implications. The proclamation of the Word is a sacramental act par excellence because it is a transforming act. It transforms the human words of the Gospel into the Word of God and the manifestation of the Kingdom. And it transforms the man who hears the Word into a receptacle of the Word and a temple of the Spirit."[29] This passage beautifully expresses the intimate and dynamic relationship of the three dimensions of initiation. The Word functions like a seed that, through the action of the Spirit, transforms creation and enables it to realize its divine potential. The result is a world which mediates, even radiates, the divine life (Trinitarian interpenetration of divine persons or *perichoresis*) through the integration of human into the divine and divine into the human. Nothing is lost of our humanity as nothing is lost of God's divinity. Both enjoy the fullness of life, and creation becomes the sacred (i.e. sacramental) playground for the divine, a type of paradise restored, only now augmented by grace into a fully sacramental shape through the aforesaid integration.

The sacramental dimension of the church, along with the liturgy which it perpetuates, can be seen as the logical outcome of the work of the Word and the Spirit. It is the result of being and remaining embodied beings as Word and Spirit act upon the created order. Sanctification means sacramentalization. It never means obliteration, except for that of sin. The work of the Word and Spirit is, then, embodied in the communal fellowship of the church, most gloriously expressed in its liturgical celebration of communion. This communion is two-fold: in the expressed love for one another in its members and in its sacramental celebration of the Eucharist. In this theological scheme, there is nothing to fear about the sacramental dimension as it poses no threat or compromise to Word or Spirit. On the contrary, it only augments Word and Spirit through sacramental expression and celebration and manifests them. As we have seen, it is only when Word and/or Spirit is neglected that problems begin to arise and the sacramental dimension begins to exert its tepid and stultifying effects devolving into a dry ritualism and a liturgy of empty gestures.

The fullness of Christian faith expressed by so many who discover the sacramental/liturgical dimension of the church after having lived in evangelical and/or charismatic churches captures well the unique gift that this dimension brings to the whole. Its various aspects serve to amplify Word and Spirit and make these dimensions tangible. Icons and sacred art and music proclaim the Word in the aesthetic beauty of its created vitality.

---

29. Schmemann, *For the Life of the World*, 33.

The liturgical calendar draws the Christian deeper into the life of Christ by participating more consciously in the seasons of his or her life. The sacraments of the church help sanctify and enliven the faithful in their journey toward God. And all of these expressions of faith help draw the faithful more concretely into God's beloved community (both on earth and in heaven), giving it a stronger sense of identity and character.

Without the sacramental dimension, then, the evangelical dimension forfeits its potential of concretizing itself in the life of the Christian community and remains unfulfilled; the pentecostal dimension faces the danger of remaining in the realm of the individual, specifically, in the individual emotions, without fully realizing the Spirit's potential for embodiment and communal formation; the intellectual dimension remains in the realm of ideas and never fully realizes that theology is meant for worship; the mystical dimension leads to Quietism and other forms of disembodied, dualistic spiritualities that do damage to the integrity of the human person; the pastoral dimension bypasses the potential for concrete expressions of affirmation and compassion that the sacraments, especially the sacraments of healing, express; the prophetic dimension would produce a church that looks more like a social organization fighting for justice than a worshiping community whose worship empowers and sends forth into the world with the ministry of reconciliation.

But with the sacramental dimension fully integrated into the life of the church, the evangelical dimension is amplified, the pentecostal dimension is embodied, the intellectual dimension moves from abstraction to reality, the mystical dimension keeps its feet on the ground, the pastoral dimension adds meaningful tools to its toolkit for ministry, and the prophetic dimension offers the poor and oppressed a place at the table in a worshiping community of equals.

More than anything, what the sacramental dimension offers the church is a source of grace and grounding. All of the witnesses for the sacramental dimension attest that God is a God intensely interested in the particularities of our everyday existence and desires to be involved in the concrete events of our created lives. The sacramental dimension helps us realize this and is the ordinary way God relates to our embodied existence. Through the conscious engagement with the sacramental dimension, the church finds the potential to be whole—body, soul, and spirit—and moves more decisively in its journey toward its final destination in God.

CHAPTER 4

The Mind of the Church
The Intellectual Dimension

SCRIPTURAL ROOTS

A paradox immediately presents itself in dealing with the biblical foundation of the intellectual dimension of the church: interpreting the place of the intellect in Judaism and Christianity from their sacred texts depends entirely on the interpreter's understanding of how these texts ought to be read—on one's hermeneutics. This conundrum illustrates just how fundamental the intellectual dimension is to religious faith and the obstacles which are created when it is ignored or marginalized.

A pre-critical reading of Sacred Scripture, ignoring the literary components of the text and critical tools for interpretation, will elicit a certain pathway of application and authoritative use of these texts in the life of the church. Engaging the text by employing critical methods will elicit quite another. Since the Bible is the foundational text for all Christian communities, a great deal depends on the acceptance or the rejection of the intellect and its capacity for engaging the text in shaping the life of the church. A great amount of ecclesial energy, Roman Catholic, Anglican, and Protestant especially, has been expended in coming to terms with the intellectual discoveries of the Bible since the beginning of the Modern period. Today, the vast majority of Roman Catholics, Anglicans, and Protestants, as well as Orthodox, have accepted an integral approach to their reading of the sacred text and fully employ literary, historical, and other critical methods in their exegesis and application for the enrichment of their ecclesial communities. Evangelical fundamentalism would be the most notable exception.

The minds of the inspired authors of the Old Testament are plainly evident throughout the vast terrain that is covered over a period of about fifteen-hundred years. The utilization of various genres, literary techniques, languages, and sophisticated narrative constructions demonstrates that from the Old Testament we observe a full display of the inspired intellect at its creative peak. A quick survey attests to this claim: the retelling of ancient Babylonian creation myths through an Israelite theological lens; the literary achievement of the Joseph cycle; the compilation of law codes that support Israel's theological convictions; the chronicling of Israel's history along a sophisticated ideological and theological vision (Deuteronomistic History); the enduring literary influence and spiritual vitality of the Psalter; the daring and creative theology of the authors of Job and Qoheleth; the profundity and striking insight of Israel's sapiential writings.

The acquisition and handing on of knowledge played a fundamental role in the preservation and development of ancient Israel. James L. Crenshaw's book *Education in Ancient Israel: Across the Deadening Silence* substantiates this truth and explores a question that will be probed in the New Testament as well as, and subsequently, throughout the history of Christianity: if truth comes from God through divine revelation, what part does humankind play in this truth's appropriation?[1] Israel's brilliance shines, for Crenshaw, in her ability to reflect on the content of her faith in order for her relationship with the divine to be appropriated in the successive generations of her long, evolving history. The experience of God, combined with the experience of the vicissitudes of life, gives birth to *theology*, the reflection on the content of faith, so that faith may be lived with integrity and God may remain in covenantal relationship with God's people from generation to generation offering them meaning and grace to enjoy life with a decisive fullness. This fullness of life, for ancient Israel, as it is for any civilization, is impossible without a cultivation of the life of the mind.

Theology is equally a driving force within the pages of the New Testament. The evangelists and authors of the epistolary literature should be understood as authors in full continuity with the theological tradition of Judaism of which most of them were a part. They were simply continuing the rich intellectual processes of the great thinkers of Judaism, only now reimagining God's truth in light of the revelation of Jesus as the crucified and risen Christ. None of the four Gospels is a straightforward rendering

---

1. James L. Crenshaw, *Education in Ancient Israel: Across the Deadening Silence* (NY: Doubleday, 1998).

of the Jesus story. Each, in their own way, at times utilizing sources, at times interjecting their own theological and literary flourishes in order to create layered narratives that combine literary ingenuity and theological insight, brought into existence a type of writing that was quite unprecedented at that time.

The dynamism of early Christianity, while largely indebted to the creative minds and inspiration of the four evangelists, is equally dependent upon the mind of St. Paul, without which Christianity would likely not have developed into the expansive movement that it did, certainly not as rapidly as it did. For Paul, the reach of the Christian movement to the ends of the earth was crucially dependent on a theological system that incorporated Jews and Gentiles into God's covenantal embrace on equal footing. This pastoral imperative unleashed the creative potential in the mind of the Apostle to the Gentiles and gave definitive shape to the church. His thought continues to enforce its influence to the present day.

The intricacy of some of his ideas, however, immediately posed problems for many of the Christians in the communities which he founded and shepherded, as is attested in several of his letters of correspondence. In fact, it was these misunderstandings that precipitated the composition of many of Paul's letters. For Paul, the ministries of pastor and teacher were intimately intertwined (cf. Eph 4:11). Thus, we see even within the pages of the New Testament the insistence on and relevance of formulating correct, well-thought out and analyzed articulations of divine revelation.

Of course, the thought of the inspired authors of the New Testament (besides Paul, special mention should be given to the anonymous author of the Epistle to the Hebrews for his magnificent achievement and to the Johannine literature whose community was likely displaced from synagogues precisely because of their theological convictions) is completely founded upon the mind of Jesus himself, their main source of inspiration. St. Paul, the four evangelists, and the other New Testament authors boldly tackled the reformulation of Israel's faith because it was imposed upon them as a divine necessity in light of the revolutionary processing that went on in the mind of Christ himself. There was no way for the early disciples of Christ to continue the Christian movement into subsequent generations without a radical rethinking of their own theological presuppositions according to the mind of Christ and his own conceptualization of God and conceptualization of his relationship to God. The effectiveness of the early Christians in their missionary expansion was not solely fueled by the power of the Spirit (the pentecostal dimension), it was equally fueled by a rationally coherent theology that Paul and the four evangelists, in particular, had assembled and convincingly argued.

DEFINING CHARACTERISTICS

We can deduce from the witness of Sacred Scripture and through what is attested to by its canonical shape and theological development the following foundational elements for the intellectual dimension of the church:

- *Theology*, the reflection on revealed truth in light of one's faith experience, *is attested to from the very beginning* of Israel's history.
- *Israel came to be a monotheistic people in the critical evaluation of her theological convictions* in relationship, mostly opposition, to the theological convictions of the pagan polytheistic systems which surrounded her.
- Within the pages of the Old Testament there is *a development of the idea of God* and sometimes *competing theologies* about God.
- *Theological diversity* is a creative tension that exists in both Old and New Testaments and is a constituent part of biblical theology.
- *The pursuit of knowledge*, for Israel, *was primarily directed toward the attainment of wisdom and right living*—living a full and honorable life in community by living righteously before the eyes of God.
- There exists a *symbiotic relationship between divine revelation and human reflection*, between faith and reason.
- Both Judaism and Christianity attest to *a high esteem for the intellect.*
- *The intellect is never an obstacle to faith* in the pages of the Bible.
- The formation of the Christian church is inconceivable without *a robust amount of critical, theological activity.*
- According to the New Testament, *theology is always done at the service of the community of believers* and is largely shaped by the church's pastoral circumstances.
- Both Old and New Testaments hold that *right living (ethics) follows right thinking.*

- The New Testament holds that *the goal of Christian existence*, the transformation of life into greater Christlikeness, *is largely dependent upon the life of the mind* (cf. Rom 12:1–2).
- The *wholeness of the church depends* in large part *in having one mind* (cf. Phil 2:2).
- *Thinking according to the mind of Christ* is one of the primary goals of Christian existence (cf. 1 Cor 2:16).

There is not a page of the Bible that isn't fully dependent upon the employment of the human intellect. It is theological through and through. It is also humanistic, thinking through and applying its theological implications to the betterment of human living. In fact, it reaches, also through theological reasoning, even to the cosmic, revealing a vision of divine and human coexistence made possible by a benevolent Creator. Made in the image and likeness of God, the human person can enter into this life-giving relationship to which the Creator calls humankind precisely because of the human intellectual capacity to do so (a point to be emphasized in the Patristic period). Relationship to the divine, then, is at least in part dependent on the human capacity to think of and imagine the divine. Just as Israel thought critically of the theological systems which surrounded her in light of her own divine revelation in order to form a unique identity for herself, so too the church continues to find her identity in like manner, depending upon both divine revelation and critical evaluation to form and maintain her sense of self. Yet, the intellect does not seek only to distinguish, it also seeks to unite, just as, in the Christian dispensation, Christ and his church seek to grow toward greater unity and catholicity, embracing the nations and welcoming all into the family of God. This movement toward inclusion is likewise founded on theological reflection in light of divine revelation.

The temptation of Marcion, seen in the light of the developmental components of biblical theology, is, then, a temptation toward anti-intellectualism and a demonstration of the poverty of a constricted intellect which would prefer to sacrifice theological tensions for a boxed-in theological ideology. The intellect is by nature open and creative, made for exploration and discovery and can never be satisfied by a simple memorization and articulation of creedal formulas and catechisms (however valuable these may be for ecclesial living).

The intellect, so understood in the Bible, seeks knowledge and wisdom in order to facilitate a specific type of living, mainly, one in accord with the precepts of God. It discriminates in order to integrate. It, therefore, bears a particular integral stamp and never for a moment moves into the realm of rationalism. It is always seen as the handmaid to ethical and spiritual living.

The intellect is, then, a bridge between the divine and the natural where the human person arbitrates and negotiates between the two. God is seeking to reign in a wildly world fallen from divine order through an intellect conformed to God's own. The human mind conformed, even transformed, by the divine imagines a world of possibility which offers the world the alternative option to self-destruction and annihilation. It is the theological imagination which saves the world by envisioning, through divine inspiration, what in the New Testament is called the Kingdom of God. In Scripture, divine and redeemed humanity work synchronistically to extend the church into all the world and help the human family mature into the mind of Christ: God, through revelation and inspiration; humankind, through theological reasoning, careful application, and bold proclamation of that theology.

Paul, the church's first great theological mind, saw clearly the intellect's role in the ingathering of all creation into the life of God. The world's transformation is a non-negotiable prerequisite, and this transformation happens through the gift of God's grace received in baptism (cf. Rom 6:1–5). Yet, the new creation given as a free gift must be appropriated and owned. The mind, for Paul, plays a crucial role in this regard: "Do not conform yourselves to this age but be transformed by the renewal of your mind, that you may discern what is the will of God, what is good and pleasing and perfect" (NABRE, Rom 12:2). Part of the good news, for Paul, is that humankind has been invited to share in the mind of Christ—a mind completely conformed to the will and knowledge of God. It is also a mind bearing certain godly characteristics. As he writes in his letter to the church at Philippi: "If there is any encouragement in Christ, any solace in love, any participation in the Spirit, any compassion and mercy, complete my joy by being of the same mind, with the same love, united in heart, thinking one thing. Do nothing out of selfishness or out of vainglory; rather, humbly regard others as more important than yourselves, each looking out not for his own interests, but [also] everyone for those of others" (NABRE, Phil 2:1–4). Having a mind unified with the mind of Christ leads to the goal of the Christian community having minds unified with one another. For Paul, to think together according to the mind of Christ is a divine mandate for the church. Notice the intimate connection in the mind of Christ, as

Paul sees it, between thinking and loving. Without the work of thinking, the work of loving is impeded. Right thinking directs the will toward right living, which, for Paul, climaxes in love—the gift of self on behalf of others. Intellect and will working as one in and according to the mind of Christ not only makes the church whole but also fosters its growth and maturation. To compromise the mind of the church is to compromise the catholicity of the church and is to compromise its mission.

THE INTELLECTUAL DIMENSION IN CHURCH HISTORY

Origen of Alexandria and the Patristic Period

At the end of the first century of the Christian era, when most of the New Testament writings would have been completed, begins what we have come to regard as the Patristic Period, commencing with the Apostolic Fathers in the first and second centuries. These Apostolic Fathers would have either known or been directly influenced by the original Apostles. Then follows the Ante-Nicene Fathers, so called because they lived before the Council of Nicea (325). The theologians of these periods all considered the life of the mind important because it was knowledge that brought the person of faith into contact with the divine. This is true of *Ignatius of Antioch* (35–108) who understood Jesus Christ as being the mind of the Father in direct continuity with the Gospel of John;[2] for *The Epistle of Diognetus* (second century) where faith and knowledge are more or less equated;[3] for *Justin Martyr* (100–165) who offers us the first exposition of Christ as Teacher;[4] for *Irenaeus of Lyons* (120–202) whose major work *Adversus haereses* never tires of warning of the dangers of erroneous doctrine and who describes God simply as Mind;[5] for *Clement of Alexandria* (150–215) who identifies the Word of God with the intellect;[6] and for *Tertullian* (160–225) who, contrary to the opinion of being one of the first Christian anti-intellectuals,

---

2. Williams, *The Divine Sense: The Intellect in Patristic Theology*, 22.
3. Williams, *The Divine Sense: The Intellect in Patristic Theology*, 23.
4. Williams, *The Divine Sense: The Intellect in Patristic Theology*, 27.
5. Williams, *The Divine Sense: The Intellect in Patristic Theology*, 23.
6. Williams, *The Divine Sense: The Intellect in Patristic Theology*, 49.

held a more fully developed understanding of what the mind was and how it functioned than all his predecessors.[7]

But it is with *Origen of Alexandria* (184–253) that we encounter the first true systematic theologian and one of the greatest minds the Christian church has ever produced. A prolific writer, Origen's output includes treatises covering a plethora of theological disciplines, including biblical exegesis and hermeneutics, apologetics, and some of the earliest works on what would be called mystical theology. The topic of the intellectual encounter with God is featured prominently in his *On First Principles* and *Contra Celsum*.

Origen's foundational idea regarding the intellect is the intellectual correspondence that exists between the divine, eternal, on the one hand, and the human, temporal, on the other.[8] Theology up until Origen tended to emphasize the distinction between divine and human, and this distinction is retained in Origen. But Origen's originality shines through with his idea of the divine-human correspondence which will open avenues for him to develop his mystical theology. Both divine transcendence and divine imminence claim their rightful place in Origen's theological system. A. N. Williams offers us justification for Origen's integral system: "God is simple intellectual nature, unspeakably surpassing all that can be thought and exceeding the power of the human mind to conceive. Nevertheless, it would be inconceivable that other minds would have any source other than God, and so, qua source of all intellectual existence, God must bear some relation to all other intellectual beings, divine transcendence notwithstanding."[9] Williams notes that both Origen's Trinitarian theology and Christology are heavily dependent upon his stress on mind.[10] This stress on mind is also a hallmark of Origen's anthropology, as is particularly emphasized in his insistence that it is the intellect above all that gives the human person divine likeness and bears the divine image. For Origen, human beings are made to be knowers and this knowledge includes the knowledge of the divine.[11] The human person's participation in the life of the Trinity (his mystical theology) is not solely an intellectual exercise; for Origen, mind and will work in

---

7. Williams, *The Divine Sense: The Intellect in Patristic Theology*, 37.
8. Williams, *The Divine Sense: The Intellect in Patristic Theology*, 45.
9. Williams, *The Divine Sense: The Intellect in Patristic Theology*, 45.
10. Williams, *The Divine Sense: The Intellect in Patristic Theology*, 46.
11. Williams, *The Divine Sense: The Intellect in Patristic Theology*, 51.

tandem to allow grace to function to full capacity in the life of the believer.[12] Love, thus, features prominently in Origen's theological vision and grounds his intellectualism in concrete expressions of life.

Criticism has been leveled at Origen for his supposed intellectualism and elitist notions among various peoples. He bluntly remarks that it is not just anyone who can partake of divine wisdom; it is only for those who are able to make distinctions between the sensible and the intelligible which is not in the capacity of all equally.[13] Origen's elitism is somewhat tempered, though, by his insistence of the need to preach the gospel to "all sorts of conditions" of people.[14] "Let the educated, the wise and the discerning come," he writes, "but let the uneducated, the ignorant and the boorish come also; for the Logos promises them healing, if they will only come, and makes all worthy of God."[15]

Criticism has also been leveled at Origen for the way he employs philosophical categories and techniques for his theological argumentation. This criticism, of course, will be a repeated concern for years to come in the ongoing history of Christian thought. But Origen insists on the gracing of mind in its pursuit of theological truth, thus, sanctifying philosophy to become an adequate helpmate for the greater and more noble pursuit of theology. He is aware of this controversial approach and offers St. Paul as an example of one who did not shy away from rational argumentation out of fear that it would separate us from Christ.[16]

The apex of Christian life for Origen is found in the contemplation of the divine. Yet, contemplation is not only the summit reached by the Christian, it is equally the path the Christian walks to get there.[17] Yet, Origen's exalted esteem for contemplation can betray his otherwise integral vision of divine and human realities. His otherworldliness gives the impression that nothing here on earth is worthy of consideration or affection. The physical senses are spiritualized and, in Origen's mind, elevated to the attainment of what truly matters, not the physical and temporal world, but the spiritual and eternal world. Yet, is such an admonition from Origen at variance from St. Paul when he writes to the Colossians: "If then you were raised with

---

12. Williams, *The Divine Sense: The Intellect in Patristic Theology*, 52.
13. Williams, *The Divine Sense: The Intellect in Patristic Theology*, 57.
14. Williams, *The Divine Sense: The Intellect in Patristic Theology*, 58.
15. Quoted in Williams, *The Divine Sense: The Intellect in Patristic Theology*, 58.
16. Williams, *The Divine Sense: The Intellect in Patristic Theology*, 64.
17. Williams, *The Divine Sense: The Intellect in Patristic Theology*, 81.

Christ, seek what is above, where Christ is seated at the right hand of God. Think of what is above, not of what is on earth. For you have died, and your life is hidden with Christ in God" (NABRE, Col 3:1–3)?

Origen's theology and ideas about the intellect would have pervasive influence on the rest of the Patristic Period, although often veiled because of the condemnations that were eventually leveled at some of his propositions. We see them in later generations as they grappled with some of the same vexing theological issues of their day. Origen remained an all-pervasive presence. Whether subsequent theologians found themselves in agreement with him or in opposition, Origen was a presence who would simply not go away. In a way, he unlocked multitudes for which future theologians could go in and explore. This they did . . . and still do.

Some of the most seminal explorers were *St. Gregory of Nazianzen* (329–390) and *St. Gregory of Nyssa* (335–395), the great Cappodocians of the fourth century. Of course, *St. Augustine*, also of the fourth century. And the monastic writers of the Egyptian desert, *Evagrius Ponticus* (345–399) and *St. John Cassian* (360–435), who gave expression to Origen's mystical theology in a new key and provided the ascetical tradition with spiritual and theological sustenance for centuries.

One of the notable and most admirable features of the patristic approach to theology was its integral nature. There is no tendency for compartmentalization; no need to separate theology and spirituality; mind and heart. The whole person was in pursuit of God and sought communion with the divine. The fracturing of intellect and will from one another will gradually begin occurring in the centuries ahead when less integral approaches of theology appear. Yet, there has always remained a remnant of those who insist on seeking God with head and heart as one. Perhaps one of the reasons for the resurgence of interest in the patristic sources of the church today is precisely because of this integral vision.

St. Thomas Aquinas and Scholasticism

The familiar quote of E. F. Hutton, "Inquiring minds want to know," may be an apt phrase to capture the spirit of the medieval mind. The patristic mind also wanted to know and, in fact, did come to know a great deal. Through immense intellectual effort, the patristic mind wrestled with and resolved some of the great theological questions set upon the mind of the church. Perhaps it is because these foundational questions had been largely settled that the medieval mind could have the leisure to explore the implications of these foundational truths to the extent that it did. Yet, what distinguishes the patristic and scholastic minds most is not the content of theological exploration as much as the method. Scholasticism as an approach to discerning the truth was first laid down by *Boethius* (477–524) in his philosophical and theological writings and then later in the eleventh century by *Peter Abalard, Lanfranc* and *St. Anselm of Canterbury*, often considered the "father of scholasticism." The scholastic method, unlike the patristic which launched its theological ruminations from the ground of Sacred Scripture and reflected symbolically, launched its theological ruminations from the broader ground of both scripture and philosophy and argued, more than reflected, methodically and analytically to formulate the most precise articulation of the truth possible. While the patristic approach was certainly not devoid of the influence of philosophy, indeed Plato and Neoplatonism heavily influenced it (some might say weighed it down), philosophy as an analytical approach to truth-finding did not incorporate itself into the patristic methodology as it would with scholasticism. The battles between St. Bernard of Clairvaux ("The Last of the Fathers") and Abelard illustrate the clash of approaches. What Bernard feared was the waywardness he perceived Abelard's intellectualism was leading him and the others who followed him. The intellectualism of Abelard, in Bernard's mind, was too imbued with the sin of pride and could not attain true knowledge of God which is only known by going the way of the ladder of humility. Bernard was, by no means, an anti-intellectualist. The clash was not about the good or evil of the intellect; it was about the place of the intellect in one's search for God. It must be remembered that Abelard would spend much of his life as a monk, devoting himself to a life of prayer. St. Anselm spent nearly his entire life as a monk. What strikes the reader of Abelard and Anselm, in juxtaposition to Bernard, is the analytical precision found in the former and the affectivity found in the latter. With scholasticism arises the question of the place of faith in the attainment of the knowledge of God. Can God be known apart from faith? What kind of knowledge of God is known by one who arrives at such knowledge through philosophical disputation yet doesn't necessarily believe what one argues? It also must be noted that neither Abelard nor Anselm approached the task of theology so grotesquely characterized. In fact, it was such a concern that led Anselm to articulate his most famous phrase: *credo ut intelligam*. Yet, what Bernard intuited, and vehemently warned against, was what he perceived as the beginning of the separation of mind from heart and will—of reason from faith. To a certain degree his concerns were justified. But, read from another angle, so were the concerns of Abelard and Anselm.

The apex of the scholastic approach was reached in one who was ironically called for a good portion of his life, the Dumb-Ox. *St. Thomas Aquinas's* (1225–1274) greatest achievement was distilled in his multi-volume *Summa Theologiae*, a theological compendium exploring from every possible angle the theological questions on the medieval mind. Taking his cue from his mentor *St. Albertus Magnus* (before 1200–1280), what separated Thomas from not only the patristic proclivities for Plato but also from the scholastics who preceded both him and his mentor, was Thomas's embrace of Aristotle. This move proved to be quite revolutionary and highly controversial with lasting implications for the life of the church and would definitively alter her shape. G. K. Chesterton, in his brilliant and revelatory biography of St. Thomas, draws parallels between the Dominican Thomas and the original Fransciscan, St. Francis. Taking them together, Chesterton paints a portrait of the mind and heart of the Middle Ages. Their unique contribution was their validation and blessing of the senses. At this point in history, for Chesterton, the church became truly Christian. No one can express this insight quite like Chesterton himself:

> In a word, St. Thomas was making Christendom more Christian in making it more Aristotelian. This is not a paradox but a plain truism, which can only be missed by those who may know what is meant by an Aristotelian, but have simply forgotten what is meant by a Christian. As compared with a Jew, a Moslem, a Buddhist, a Deist, or most obvious alternatives, a Christian *means* a man who believes that deity or sanctity has attached to matter or entered the world of the senses. Some modern writers, missing this simple point, have even talked as if the acceptance of Aristotle was a sort of concession to the Arabs; like a Modernist vicar making a concession to the Agnostics. They might as well say that the Crusades were a concession to the Arabs as say that Aquinas rescuing Aristotle from Averrhoes was a concession to the Arabs. The Crusaders wanted to recover the place where the body of Christ had been, because they believed, rightly or wrongly, that it was a Christian place. St. Thomas wanted to recover what was in essence the body of Christ itself; the sanctified body of the Son of Man which had become a miraculous medium between heaven and earth. And he wanted the body, and all its senses, because he believed, rightly or wrongly, that it was a Christian thing. It might be a humbler or

homelier thing than the Platonic mind; that is why it was Christian. St. Thomas was, if you will, taking the lower road when he walked in the steps of Aristotle. So was God, when He worked in the workshop of Joseph.[18]

It would be a gross misjudgment, then, to depict Thomas's scholasticism as a form of rationalism lost in abstraction separated from the real. Thomas, in fact, was a realist completely liberated in mind because the mind was created by God for the precise reason of knowing God within the milieu of the created world. The criticism that intellectual abstraction distances the self from the concrete reality of the whole by an endless pursuit of dissecting the whole into pieces fails, according to Thomas, because the intellect has the capacity to both think in wholes and in parts. To ignore the parts that make up the whole is, in Thomas's mind, to ultimately miss the whole. For Thomas and the scholastics in general, the intellect's task is precisely to connect the pieces of the puzzle and organize it into a systematic whole. Reality is missed without this intellectual adventure. Without the work of the intellect, disparities remain disparities, contradictions remain contradictions. With the intellect's power "otherness" is overcome and reality is augmented in the communion of opposites or in what was once thought so to be. The intellect, then, for St. Thomas, is an integrating faculty bestowing understanding and insight into what is of greater possibility in the area of the real. It makes the real more real . . . or more really understood and known . . . and thereby possibly lived and enjoyed.

The criticism frequently leveled at scholasticism as a theological approach is that it is overly abstract, too dependent upon philosophical categories rather than biblical theology, and operates from a too high esteem of the intellect and its ability to reach divine realities apart from faith and matters of the heart. What results, from these critics' perspective, is hair splitting speculation about what can't ultimately be known and for what has little relevance to life, even if it could be known. It is a waste of time and a misguided quest—even one filled with hubris and intellectual arrogance. Such a characterization is certainly not the life and thought of St. Thomas Aquinas and for many others working within this paradigm of theological enquiry and is generally an unhelpful and dismissive way of unnecessarily throwing the baby out with the bathwater. Criticism has been legitimate, however, to the extent that the intellectual quest for the divine in the scholastic method failed to integrate the life of faith along with its

18. Chesterton, *Saint Thomas Aquinas: The Dumb Ox*, 21–22.

intellectual interests. Because more philosophical methods became available to the inquiring mind of the Middle Ages, it became possible to approach questions about the divine in purely philosophical categories. It was not an inevitable choice and most did not reach such an extreme approach but some certainly did teeter along the precipice and failed to adequately demonstrate the significance of their disputed questions and answers with Christian living. Up until this moment in the life of the church, theology was at the service of the church. Now, theology became possible to serve its own end.

Many reformers of the late Medieval and Reformation periods were motivated to work toward securing the union of mind and heart. *John Wycliffe* (1330–1384) and *Jan Hus* (1370/71–1415) were two notable reformers whose efforts caused much controversy and were vehemently squashed by the Roman Catholic Church. *John Gerson* (1363–1429), on the other hand, managed to affect a more acceptable change. His emphasis on scripture and affective theology and criticism of dry, university intellectualism became barometers around which to chart forth his work of reform. As Ulrich Leinsle explains, according to Gerson, "Theology should again serve the purpose of human life, eternal salvation, for man aspires to God as his natural center and place of rest. This is where certainty can be found with regard to Scholastic disputes and the insecurity of theological knowledge. Therefore theology must immediately become a biblical, affective, mystical theology in which theory and practice are united."[19]

Anti-scholastic movements began to form as well. One of the most important was led by *Geert Groote* (1340–1384) and the movement he inspired, the *devotio moderna*. Groote wanted more than anything a reform that would take the church back to the early Christian period with simplicity of focus upon the following of Christ in faithful discipleship. He repudiated the scholastic method of disputation and, inspired by Gerson, sought to unite the intellectualism of the schools with the pastoral concerns of the local churches.

Schleiermacher and Barth

Two of the most significant post-Reformation responses to the question of the place of the intellect in the life of the church came from Protestants

---

19. Leinsle, *Introduction to Scholastic Theology*, 201–02.

seeking further reform in their own proper historical contexts: *Friedrich Schleiermacher* (1768–1834) and *Karl Barth* (1886–1968).

Schleiermacher, often referred to as the father of Protestant liberalism, did more than, perhaps, any other theologian to bring Christianity into the modern world. Influenced by the Enlightenment philosophers of his day, especially Kant, Fichte, and Hegel, he was a modern man through and through.[20] One of Schleiermacher's aims was to foster a Christian consciousness that would be an answer to an Enlightenment generation that had become weary of religion and "to reweave religion, threatened with oblivion, into the incomparably rich fabric of the burgeoning intellectual life of modern times."[21] Schleiermacher promoted the "positive" element in religion which placed emphasis on how the infinite can be grasped only in the multitude of forms in which it manifests itself. The mind cannot grasp the "Infinite" in itself. He also placed great emphasis on the phenomenology and psychology of religion where experience of one's absolute dependence upon the "Infinite" becomes a prerequisite for the knowledge of God and forms the essence of Christian faith. With this dual focus upon intellect and emotion, Schleiermacher, according to Richard Crouter, is best situated between the Enlightenment and Romanticism.[22] Crouter understands Schleiermacher as an integral figure within the permeable boundaries of these two periods.

It is common to depict Barth and the Neo-orthodox movement he inspired largely as a response to Schleiermacher and the theological liberalism that rose in his wake. Although Crouter criticizes this perspective as overdrawn, the basis of the argument is that liberal Protestantism since Schleiermacher "had orientated itself completely on pious, religious human beings instead of on God and his revelation . . ." and ". . . had come to an arrangement in uncritical assimilation to the ruling political systems of their time."[23] Because of the implications of such a perspective in the milieu of National Socialism, Barth insisted that a stand had to be made.[24] Barth's theology stands, then, on two legs: on the leg of theological inquiry

---

20. Küng, *Great Christian Thinkers*, 161.

21. Quote of Rudolph Otto from his Introduction to *On Religion* in Küng, *Great Christian Thinkers*, 166.

22. See Crouter, *Friedrich Schleiermacher: Between Enlightenment and Romanticism*.

23. Crouter, *Friedrich Schleiermacher: Between Enlightenment and Romanticism*, 191–92.

24. Crouter, *Friedrich Schleiermacher: Between Enlightenment and Romanticism*, 192.

in a Neo-orthodox vein, on the one hand, and on the leg of practical theology, on the other. Barth's significance, in this regard, has been universally acknowledged by both Protestants and Catholics alike. The late Hans Küng, a Roman Catholic, notes the following long-lasting "great intentions" of his fellow Swiss theologian:

- The biblical texts are not mere documents of philological–historical research but make possible an encounter with the 'wholly other'; the utterly human testimonies of the Bible are concerned with God's Word, which men and women can acknowledge, know, and confess.

- Men and women are thus called to more than neutral contemplation and interpretation: their penitence, conversion and faith is required, a faith which always remains a venture; human salvation and damnation are at stake here.

- It is the task of the church to express uncompromisingly in society, through its human words, this word of God on which men and women can always rely in trust.[25]

Küng, along with Hans Urs von Balthasar, are two prominent Roman Catholic theologians who have done much to reveal the common ground of Barth's Protestant theological vision and their own Catholicism: Küng in his work on justification and von Balthasar in his important book on Barth challenging Barth's criticisms of *analogy of faith* and demonstrating the homogeneity between the two theological perspectives. Barth was impressed with von Balthasar's work and noted that von Balthasar understood him better than most of any of his other contemporaries.

This Protestant/Catholic dialogue is only one of the many instances of authentic ecumenical exchanges that now characterize the current theological climate the church enjoys today. It gives expression to what had been established at least since the time of Aquinas, the intellect seeks to distinguish only to unite.

John Paul II's Fides et ratio

The long history of Roman Catholic thought about the relationship between faith and reason in the human quest for God coalesced in the magisterial work of John Paul II, *Fides et ratio* of 1998. It was the Holy Father's desire

25. Küng, *Great Christian Thinkers*, 201–02.

to appropriate the teaching of Vatican Council I on the place of reason in the theological endeavor for a new age. Vatican I taught, as the Holy Father explained, "that the truth attained by philosophy and the truth of Revelation are neither identical nor mutually exclusive...."[26] He, thus, begins his apostolic address by immediately focusing upon the relationship between these two ways of knowing God with this memorable and evocative statement: "Faith and reason are like two wings on which the human spirit rises to contemplation of truth; and God has placed in the human heart a desire to know the truth—in a word, to know himself—so that, by knowing and loving God, men and women may also come to the fullness of truth about themselves."[27] While the sources for this knowledge of God are multiple, the Holy Father focuses his attention on two that are most primary: philosophy and theology. Philosophy pertains to the search for wisdom mainly through rational means. Theology pertains to the reflection on Revelation. Both orient the human person toward the transcendent, and both are gifts of God luring human consciousness toward a fuller incorporation of the divine. Yet, these two means of knowledge of God are not set on an equal plain. The Holy Father reiterates the teaching of Vatican Council I: "there exists a knowledge which is peculiar to faith, surpassing the knowledge proper to human reason...."[28] This knowledge peculiar to faith appears as something utterly gratuitous giving the person of faith a definitive glimpse of the divine. Yet it can never be separated from the working of the intellect, which itself is a gift of the divine directed toward theological knowledge. *Fides et ratio*, thus, sets forth an integral, epistemological vision. As the Holy Father expresses when speaking of this integral relationship between faith and reason, "each contains the other, and each has its own scope for action."[29] Militating against extreme ideological perspectives, faith and reason's integral nature also steer the Christian on a balanced pathway toward God. The church is thus protected from both rationalism (reason without faith) and fideism (faith without reason), the two cliffs along the theological journey.

In Chapter VI, "The Interaction between Philosophy and Theology," the Holy Father demonstrates the demands of philosophical reason for the knowledge of faith. *Fides et ratio* insists that the mind of the believer must

26. John Paul II, *Fides et ratio*.
27. John Paul II, *Fides et ratio*.
28. John Paul II, *Fides et ratio*.
29. John Paul II, *Fides et ratio*.

acquire a natural, consistent, and true knowledge of created realities, both of the world and humankind together. Without this intellectual pursuit aimed at a clear understanding of reality in its objective form, the mind's capacity for a proper understanding of God through faith will be compromised and limp along with a fragmented frame of reference. The subjective world of faith needs the objective world of reason upon which to stand.

The intellect, therefore, plays a foundational role in the life of the church for Roman Catholics, as is articulated in this authoritative document. Yet, the intellect is never enough in and of itself to attain the knowledge of God. It is, rather, constituted integrally with faith and serves as faith's coordinating system from which the human spirit rises to the contemplation of the truth.

The Anti-Intellectualism of Fundamentalism

In Mark Noll's book *The Scandal of the Evangelical Mind,* the evangelical historian affirmatively quotes Dr. Os Guinness assessing American evangelicalism's anti-intellectual tendencies.

> Evangelicals have been deeply sinful in being anti-intellectual ever since the 1820s and 1830s. For the longest time we didn't pay the cultural price for that because we had the numbers, the social zeal, and the spiritual passion for the gospel. But today we are beginning to pay the cultural price. And you can see that most evangelicals simply don't think. For example, there has been no serious evangelical public philosophy in this century . . . . It has always been a sin not to love the Lord our God with our minds as well as our hearts and souls . . . . We have excused this with a degree of pietism and pretend that this is something other than what it is—that is, sin . . . . Evangelicals need to repent of their refusal to think Christianly and to develop the mind of Christ.[30]

Noll sees the current anti-intellectual bent of evangelicals as an unfortunate betrayal of the rich intellectual heritage of early evangelicalism, especially since Jonathan Edwards, perhaps evangelicalism's most important source of inspiration. For Noll, contemporary evangelicals are fashioning themselves too much like the Albigenses who slighted formal intellectual labor and undervalued the life of the mind and like the Pietists whose thrust "was to draw believers back from formal, dogmatic rigidity toward living Christian

---

30. Cited in Noll, *The Scandal of the Evangelical Mind*, 23.

experience."³¹ Noll properly critiques this approach for its lack of integral reciprocity: "A problem arises . . . when a necessary means of renewal becomes the sum of the faith, when a part of more general Christian life dominates the whole."³²

Historically, Noll sees the breakdown of the intellectual mind among evangelicals, since Edwards, taking place during the period of the Great Revivals. As he states, "Revivals called people to Christ as a way of escaping tradition, including traditional learning."³³ With the rise of dispensationalism, fundamentalism's effort at being intellectual, many evangelicals, according to Noll, got pigeon-holed in "the most disastrous effects on the mind."³⁴ Instead of intellectually engaging the world with the implications of the gospel, evangelicalism found itself preoccupied with curious scenarios of Christ's return and the vagaries of end-time prophecy. Later, it would be marked by defensive strategies against science and modernist approaches to scripture. All these forces would cause evangelicals of the twentieth century to hunker down in isolation, setting its roots deeper in the soil of an either/or, dualistic consciousness.

Evangelicalism in the late twentieth century has opened itself in various ways to correcting its anti-intellectual past. Noll points to Billy Graham and, especially, to C. S. Lewis, whose seminal writings influenced so many, as twentieth-century figures who have shown the way of being both evangelical and intellectual.

Richard Hofstadter's 1964 Pulitzer Prize-winning book *Anti-Intellectualism in American Life* also blames evangelicalism for a great deal of America's ongoing anti-intellectualist tendencies. Pointing to the early English reformers who exerted so much influence in shaping the religious ethos of early America, Hofstadter sees their radical positioning against the main spokesmen of the Reformation, who they assessed did not go far enough in dealing with the social and spiritual changes desired by many, as leading to successive waves of Millennarians, Anabaptists, Seekers, Ranters, and Quakers assailing the established order and its clergy, preaching a religion of the poor, arguing for intuition and inspiration as against learning and doctrine, elevating lay preachers to leadership, and rejecting the

---

31. Noll, *The Scandal of the Evangelical Mind*, 47.
32. Noll, *The Scandal of the Evangelical Mind*, 49.
33. Noll, *The Scandal of the Evangelical Mind*, 63.
34. Noll, *The Scandal of the Evangelical Mind*, 132.

professional clergy as null and void and without authority.[35] Like Noll, Hofstedter also sees Revivalism as only making things worse for the life of the mind in evangelicalism. Subsequently, "The Puritan ideal of the minister as an intellectual and educational leader was steadily weakened in the face of the evangelical ideal of the minister as a popular crusader and exhorter."[36] During this time, "Theological education itself became more instrumental. Simple dogmatic formulations were considered sufficient. In considerable measure the churches withdrew from intellectual encounters with the secular world, gave up the idea that religion is a part of the whole life of intellectual experience, and often abandoned the field of rational studies on the assumption that they were the natural province of science alone."[37] Then, by 1853, Bela Bates Edwards, one of the outstanding clergymen of his day, could complain that there was "an impression, somewhat general, that an intellectual clergyman is deficient in piety, and that an eminently pious minister is deficient in intellect."[38] Along with Noll, Hofstedter reads evangelicalism's wrestling with modernism as only stunting evangelicalism's intellectual capacities.

Fundamentalism, the extreme, militant wing of evangelicalism, would thus increasingly identify itself more and more by what it was against than what it was for. In doing so, it dug itself deeper and deeper into its own trenches unwilling to budge from its self-assured perspectives. It became increasingly isolationist and less catholic. Hofstedter assesses fundamentalism's tendencies toward absolutizing with particular clarity: "The fundamentalist mind . . . is essentially Manichean; it looks upon the world as an arena for conflict between absolute good and absolute evil, and accordingly it scorns compromises (who would compromise with Satan?) and can tolerate no ambiguities. It cannot find serious importance in what it believes to be trifling degrees of difference . . . ."[39]

Hofstedter does not reserve his critique to Protestant fundamentalism alone. He also takes aim at American Catholicism for helping contribute to America's anti-intellectual consciousness: "American Catholicism has devoted itself alternately to denouncing the aspects of American life it could not approve and imitating more acceptable aspects in order to surmount its

---

35. Hofstedter, *Anti-Intellectualism in American Life*, 57.
36. Hofstedter, *Anti-Intellectualism in American Life*, 86.
37. Hofstedter, *Anti-Intellectualism in American Life*, 86.
38. Hofstedter, *Anti-Intellectualism in American Life*, 87.
39. Hofstedter, *Anti-Intellectualism in American Life*, 135.

minority complex and 'Americanize' itself. In consequence, the American Church ... lacks an intellectual culture."[40] For Hofstedter, this is in spite of the number of Catholic colleges and universities which exist throughout the country, to which he gives a low grade: "The intellectual achievement of Catholic colleges and universities remains startlingly low, both in the sciences and in the humanities."[41] Catholicism, for Hofstedter, also mirrored Protestant fundamentalism in its response to modernity: "... a great many Catholics have been as responsive as Protestant fundamentalists to that revolt against modernity of which I have spoken, and they have done perhaps more than their share in developing the one-hundred percent mentality."[42] Hofstedter highlights the irony of this Catholic/Protestant coalition against all things modern:

> Indeed, one of the most striking developments of our time has been the emergence of a kind of union, or at least a capacity for cooperation, between Protestant and Catholic fundamentalists, who share a common puritanism and a common mindless militance on what they imagine to be political issues, which unite them in opposition to what they repetitively call Godless Communism. Many Catholics seem to have overcome the natural reluctance one might expect them to have to join hands with the very type of bigoted Protestant who scourged their ancestors. It seems a melancholy irony that a union which the common bonds of Christian fraternity could not achieve has been forged by the ecumenicism of hatred.[43]

Even if Hofstedter's perspective is weighed down with ideological stridency, both Protestantism and Roman Catholicism struggle in their own ways with the shadowside of militant absolutism which threatens to co-op a truly catholic consciousness. Divisiveness in each of these communities has resulted from this polarizing, either/or approach and disunity, even within particular local communities, has become one of the greatest sins of the contemporary church. This is the case within the Roman Catholic Church even in spite of the efforts of Vatican II to cautiously adapt itself to the modern world. It can be argued that, from a young ultra-conservative Roman Catholic's perspective, Vatican II is largely responsible for this

---

40. Hofstedter, *Anti-Intellectualism in American Life*, 136.
41. Hofstedter, *Anti-Intellectualism in American Life*, 139.
42. Hofstedter, *Anti-Intellectualism in American Life*, 140.
43. Hofstedter, *Anti-Intellectualism in American Life*, 140.

fundamentalistic trend since it is perceived that Vatican II was not a proper, judicious response to the modern world but a capitulation to it. This has been most obvious to most Roman Catholics in the renewal of the liturgy which, for some, was no renewal at all but a loss of the sense of the sacred. What has resulted is not a well-thought-out response resulting in a call for a renewed liturgy with a greater sense of the sacred—in other words, to keep renewing the liturgy—but a reversal of any semblance of renewal at all and a call to return to "the extraordinary form." This move, like so many in fundamentalistic responses, is largely uncritical, emotional, and reactionary—evidence of the severing of mind and heart.

TOWARD AN INTEGRAL INTELLECTUAL ECCLESIAL SHAPE

From the historical outline above, the precarious position of the intellect in ecclesial life stands out as one of the greatest storylines of Christian history. What is at the center of this struggle for mind and heart to remain whole and intact is, it seems, the question of our conceptualization of the fundamental nature of the divine. If God for us is purely Spirit and power to save, then Christian life will be mostly about the experience of liberation (like it is for many evangelicals and pentecostals). If God for us is purely a divine mind revealing hidden truths to a rational, well-ordered world, then Christian life will be mostly about rationally discovering these hidden truths and appropriating them to human life. But God is both power and revelation and humankind is both liberated and transformed through evangelical, pentecostal encounter and intellectual appropriation. Can the reason why so many evangelicals and pentecostals get stuck in their particular ecclesial worlds be because encounter is a lot easier than the life-long wrestling with the truth? Yet, without the hard work of discerning and appropriating divinely revealed truths, the church is left statically existing in a world which simply no longer speaks the same language as it and, therefore, cannot be understood. There is something woefully unevangelical about this . . . and uncatholic.

Without the intellectual dimension of the church intact, the evangelical dimension falters into the isolationism of fundamentalism and the pentecostal dimension becomes fixated on its own power and too often mistakes charisma for theological depth and gets stuck in superficial spirituality. The intellectual dimension grounds the mystical dimension in the soil of reality and keeps the mystic on the right course toward what ultimately transcends human intelligence. It, likewise, enlivens the sacramental/liturgical dimension with its hidden potential for enrichment (how many well-intentioned Christians miss out on the transformative power of the liturgy because they inadequately understand the liturgy's prayers, gestures, and symbolic significance?). Intelligence, especially emotional intelligence, offers a refined intuition and a greater capacity for effective pastoral ministry and keeps the minister from falling into the rut of uncreative and monotonous—and largely untransformative—service. The intellectual dimension, finally, prevents the church's prophetic dimension from succumbing to the ideological liberalism that finds its foundation not in well-reasoned strategy for a just social order but in a shortsighted form of compassion that, in the long run, fails to truly liberate.

CHAPTER 5

The Heart of the Church
The Mystical Dimension

SCRIPTURAL ROOTS

From the first pages of God's creative acts in the Bible, it is firmly established that humankind was created to enjoy a special type of relationship with the Creator. The rest of biblical history that unfolds in Sacred Scripture is the drama of this relationship: at times threatened; at times broken; at times restored . . . on and on, the fracturing and the reconciling dynamics of this relationship are on full display and form the core plotline of the biblical narrative.

God desires to walk with Adam and Eve in the cool of the evening at one moment, and Adam and Eve are hiding from God at the next. In the age of Noah, God destroys all living things (except Noah and those he saves) only to restore the living and form a covenant with all creation. In Abraham, God further seeks to bridge the gap between human and divine through another covenant that will bestow the blessing of God's presence and provision in a unique way among all the peoples of the earth. In Moses, God binds the covenant people even closer in making the divine will known through Torah giving this people clear guidelines on how to stay close to this God who unrelentingly keeps seeking closeness. Moses, above all of the sons and daughters of Israel in the Old Testament, is the one who enjoys closest proximity to God, nowhere more vividly depicted as in the pivotal, theophanic moment on Mount Sinai where the cloud of God's glory descends upon him and leaves its blinding mark:

> When Moses came down from Mount Sinai with the two tablets of the Testimony in his hands, as he was coming down the mountain, Moses did not know that the skin of his face was radiant because he had been talking to him. And when Aaron and all the Israelites saw Moses, the skin on his face was so radiant that they were afraid to go near him. But Moses called to them, and Aaron and all the leaders of the community rejoined him, and Moses talked to them, after which all the Israelites came closer, and he passed on to them all the orders that Yahweh had given to him on Mount Sinai. Once Moses had finished speaking to them, he put a veil over his face. Whenever Moses went into Yahweh's presence to speak with him, he took the veil off until he came out. And when he came out, he would tell the Israelites what orders he had been given, and the Israelites would see Moses' face radiant. Then Moses would put the veil back over his face until he went in to speak to him next time (NJB, Exodus 34:29–35).

Along with Moses, the prophet Elijah also enjoys a similar intimacy with God. Characterized as being possessed with God's spirit, speaking and acting in the power of God and experiencing a similar theophanic encounter with God as did Moses, Elijah, on Mount Horeb (Sinai), is confronted by a mysterious "sound of sheer silence." This Moses/Elijah mountain top experience will be exploited to great effect, not only in the New Testament (in both the Transfiguration scene in the Gospels and by Paul [cf. 3:4–4:6]), but also in the patristic era, most notably in St. Gregory of Nyssa in his *Life of Moses*.

Another of the major paradoxes of scripture arises at this point in the unfolding drama: intimacy with God can never be presumed and must always be on God's terms. There are many passages within the pages of the Old Testament that attest to the dangers of getting too close to God without being adequately prepared or divinely elected. Miriam comes to mind (cf. Num 12). So does Uzzah (cf. 2 Sam 6:1–7). As does the ministry of the High Priest in the Holy of Holies on the Day of Atonement (cf. Lev 16). The holiness of God is such an overriding theme in the Old Testament that it has had the tendency to impose itself and dominate the overall theology of the Old Testament and to, at times, overshadow the theology of covenant. One may ask: Does God want to be close to us or not? Is God's holiness (which literally means "to be separate") a negation of intimacy? Are the holiness of God and God's desire for a covenantal bond contradictory and irreconcilable themes in the Old Testament?

These themes of holiness and covenant create a lively tension within the sacred text that gives rise to a creative theological tradition which will never fully allow one truth to eclipse the other. An integral vision will develop that both the prophetic and wisdom literature, and then the New Testament, will creatively expound.

The demands of holiness are firmly established in the prophetic literature. One may get the impression that the God of Israel is a God to be feared rather than loved, but a close reading of the Prophets paints a picture of a God who is to be feared in order that God's chosen and elect may enjoy the blessings of the covenantal bond and know God's love. Israel is to be separate from the nations in order to remain bound to God. Holiness is the prerequisite to relationship and is a means to the end which is the covenantal bond. After many years of drilling the need for holiness into the hearts and minds of a people prone to idolatry (often imaged in the prostitute cheaply binding herself to whatever immediately satisfies . . . a form of false intimacy), a prophet will arise in the sixth century exilic period with a message notably distinct from the prophets of doom preceding him. Second Isaiah, as he has come to be known, bore a message which was unapologetically encouraging and comforting. This prophet, acutely in tune with the devastating difficulties of God's people in exile, offered a vision of God of breathtaking beauty. As this beleaguered people understandably doubted whether the covenantal bond remained at all, Second Isaiah would say:

> And now, thus says Yahweh,
> he who created you, Jacob,
> who formed you, Israel:
> Do not be afraid, for I have redeemed you;
> I have called you by your name, you are mine.
> Should you pass through the waters, I shall be with you;
> or through rivers, they will not swallow you up.
> Should you walk through fire, you will not suffer,
> And the flame will not burn you.
> For I am Yahweh, your God,
> the Holy One of Israel, your Saviour (NJB, Isaiah 43:1–3a).

Years later in the Isaiah tradition we are offered another striking image of intimacy:

> Rejoice with Jerusalem,
> be glad for her, all you who love her!

> Rejoice, rejoice with her,
> all you who mourned her!
> So that you may be suckled and satisfied
> from her consoling breast,
> so that you may drink deep with delight
> from her generous nipple (NJB, Isaiah 66:10–11).[1]

The entirety of The Song of Songs was interpreted in ancient Israel as an allegory of God's love for Israel, a wildly passionate love. The epilogue to the work captures the drama between the two human lovers and grounds their love in the divine:

> Set me like a seal on your heart,
> like a seal on your arm.
> For love is strong as Death,
> passion as relentless as Sheol.
> The flash of it is a flash of fire,
> a flame of Yahweh himself.
> Love no flood can quench,
> no torrents drown.
> Were a man to offer all his family wealth
> to buy love,
> contempt is all that he would gain (NJB, Song of Songs 8:6–7).

Likely written in the first century BCE, the Wisdom of Solomon characterizes wisdom as an attribute of the divine that is shared with the human and further binds the two, human and divine, together in perpetuity:

> Wisdom I loved and searched for from my youth;
> I resolved to have her as my bride,
> I fell in love with her beauty.
> She enhances her noble birth by sharing God's life,
> for the Master of All has always loved her.
> Indeed, she shares the secrets of God's knowledge,
> and she chooses what he will do (NJB, Wisdom of Solomon 8:2–4).
> I therefore determined to take her to share my life,
> knowing that she would be my counsellor in prosperity
> and comfort me in cares and sorrow (NJB, Wisdom of Solomon 8:9).
> By means of her, immortality will be mine (NJB, Wisdom of Solomon 8:13a).

With this quick survey of Old Testament texts, a particular strain which highlights a theology where Israel's God is not only approachable,

---

1. For a similar maternal image of God, also see Psalm 131.

but also vulnerable and full of desire, appears—a theology which is strikingly distinct from any of the other polytheistic traditions of the Ancient Near East. In addition to the consoling image of God painted by these texts, a hope for a Messiah would be prophesied and express the deepest longing of Israel and her most daring intuition for the possibilities of human and divine intimacy. The New Testament is an account of the fulfillment of this intuition and hope.

Jesus of Nazareth, who came to be understood by his followers as the fulfillment of this Messianic hope, is depicted in the Gospels as the faithful Israelite who enjoyed a proximity to God heretofore unseen. Much of the energy of the Evangelists is spent on exploring precisely what kind of relationship this entailed and on the ultimate identity of Jesus in relation to God. He speaks and acts like a prophet but doesn't seem to be able to be contained within the confines of a prophetic category. He speaks as a great wisdom teacher but is considered to be more than a sage. Beyond prophet and sage, he is deemed a Son . . . God's unique and only-begotten Son . . . not only by those who came to believe him to be so but also by God at both Jesus' baptism and transfiguration. The Transfiguration of Jesus on Mount Tabor not only serves to reveal the identity of Jesus as Son of God but also manifests the eschatological glory of the reign of God in Jesus' person . . . a vision not only of what is to come but also of what is the deepest reality of the here and now. The two figures of the Old Testament who enjoyed the closest proximity to God (Moses and Elijah) now disappear and the glorified Jesus alone is left. The former glory has passed away and a far greater glory has appeared (cf. 2 Cor 3:11). Yet, this manifest glory cannot remain for long, for Jesus must continue his journey to the cross where, especially according to the Gospel of John, Jesus' glory will be most gloriously revealed and now shared with those who believe. In Jesus' resurrection from the dead, he is vindicated by God and proven truly to be the unique and only-begotten Son as he said, and, in the process, opens up access to God in a new and definitive way, dramatically depicted in the tearing of the veil of the sanctuary from top to bottom (cf. Matt 27:51).

The Gospel of Luke also presents two scenes which have nurtured the mystical dimension of the church through the centuries, both emphasizing very similar aspects of this dimension. The first is the Annunciation of Mary embedded in the Infancy Narrative; the second is the story of Mary and Martha (cf. Luke 10:38–42). Each depicts the proper disposition of the model disciple as listening attentively and pondering deeply.

The theophanic encounter of Mary with the Angel Gabriel and the startling news that she will bear the Son of God as the Holy Spirit overshadows her is later treasured and pondered in the heart so as to penetrate more deeply her new, mysterious reality. Mary of Bethany's choice to sit and listen at Jesus' feet, rather than Martha's choice to be busy about many things, serves to highlight the preeminent posture of contemplative listening and adoration over anxious distraction, even when the distracted work is for the Lord.

Paul of Tarsus would become the first Christian to translate what has come to be known as the Paschal Mystery (the dying and rising of Christ) into a theological vision. Paul should be read as a pastoral theologian (not a systematic one) who is trying to help the Christian understand the implications of the Paschal Mystery for their lives. Since Albert Schweizer's seminal study, *The Mysticism of Paul the Apostle*, published in 1930, Pauline theology has taken more seriously an alternative reading of Luther and the traditional Protestant interpretation of Paul. It is not a mysticism of the blurring of identities between human and divine but one of the transformation of the self through the Christian's identification with Christ, most precisely in his death and resurrection, experienced through participation in various ways: faith; sacraments; experience. For Paul, the Christian who professes faith in Christ is baptized into his death and begins a life of participation in the new creation offered by grace. This resurrected mode of existence is a sharing in the risen life of Christ who now reigns in power with God. The Christian is now hidden with Christ in God and is to seek the things that are above where his/her true life now reigns with Christ (cf. Col 3:1–3). A definitive change and reconstitution has been effected through faith and sacrament, and the Christian is now "in Christ." The sinful influences of the old self may still exert their power, but the Christian must put those influences to death by setting one's mind and heart and "members" on Christ who will exert his greater power over them and keep the Christian from sin and preserve him/her in holiness and intimacy with God. For Paul, the revolutionary event of the Paschal Mystery has made God no longer a God to be related to in a purely objective manner, God is now also a subjective reality within the heart of the Christian who is to now live, move, and act from the sanctuary of the heart.

Paul's mystical theology finds its basis not only in his carefully worked out ideas about the Christian's relationship to God in Christ but also in his first-hand encounters with the risen Lord, his being caught up to the "third heaven," and the numerous revelations he purports to have had, citations scattered throughout the Pauline literature and the Acts of the Apostles. It should also be noted that Paul spent three years in the Arabian desert, presumably meditating on his experience of God in Christ, before beginning his apostolic ministry.

The Johannine literature has a notably mystical bent as well, although painting in quite different shades than Paul. Love, for John, best characterizes the divine reality and is the content of God. This love is the Spirit that enters into the human heart and binds all together: divine and human and humankind with each other. The author of the book of Revelation sees a realm of existence where a new heaven and a new earth make it possible for God to dwell with humankind . . . like in the Garden of Eden but now in eschatological fulfillment: "Look, here God lives among human beings. He will make his home among them; they will be his people, and he will be their God, God-with-them" (NJB, Rev 21:3). The whole trajectory of the biblical narrative completes its arc and finds its fulfillment in heaven and earth becoming one.

DEFINING CHARACTERISTICS

Because the mystical dimension of the church is perhaps the dimension most prone to spurn heretical movements and to be looked upon with suspicion from the several Protestant traditions who reacted (overreacted?) against it for their perceived (at times actual) neglect of scriptural foundation, it is expediently important to ground this dimension in sound biblical theology. A biblical Christian mysticism clearly emerges which will help guide the developing Christian mystical tradition as movements in the Christian church reflect upon their continuing experience of God. Some of these defining characteristics are:

- Being created in the divine image and likeness, *the human person bears an innate openness and compatibility to the divine.*
- The desire of God is *to be near* to the human person, regardless of the human person's sinful actions, expressed in God's initiative in making *covenantal bonds* with humankind.
- The God of the covenant, particularly demonstrated with Abraham and Moses, is a God who enters a relationship *characterized by intimacy and vulnerability* . . . a God who acts and desires to be acted upon.

- This same God is a God of revelation. This is most definitively depicted in the Old Testament as God reveals the divine name: *Yahweh . . . the God who is there to save.*
- The revelation of God bears an *experiential* component: Yahweh's glory is made known in a series of *theophanies.*
- The experience of the glory of God *leaves a lasting impact and transformative change* in those who experience it.
- Torah, as part of the revelation of God, functions as a gift of God to solidify the covenantal bond and *keep the people of God close* to the God who journeys and tabernacles with them.
- The holiness of God and its demands upon the people of God *serve to protect this relationship of covenantal intimacy.*
- From the experience of Elijah on Mount Horeb we learn that *God is at times encountered in the pregnant silence* beyond the order of creation.
- The *Prophets functioned to call the people of God back to covenantal relationship* and a restoration of intimacy with God. This is often depicted in the prophetic literature in God's desire to bring *comfort to those who suffer.*
- *Desire for God*, most profoundly attested to in an allegorical interpretation of The Song of Songs, plays a significant component in the cultivation of one's intimacy with God and corresponds to God's mutual desire for those who are the object of the *divine affection.*
- The *Wisdom of God is a reality which serves to bind the human to the divine.*
- In the life, death, and resurrection of Jesus of Nazareth, God has affected *a new covenantal bond with humankind* whereby the human person now has greater access to God.
- *The Holy Spirit* is the divine reality given to the person of faith to effect the changes wrought in the Paschal Mystery.
- The Spirit is definitively given in the *sacraments* to effect this change and conformity to Christ.
- The Christian, through faith and sacrament, is now found *"in Christ"* and becomes a *"new creation"* with *God dwelling in the heart.*

- Through the *contemplative pondering of the mysteries* of Christian faith and sacrament, the Christian appropriates their realities and puts them into action and embodies them through Christian living.

- God *as love* binds all things together and overcomes the darkness of sin and death *making the eschatological reign of God a present reality* to be known and lived.

Bernard McGinn, the preeminent scholar of Christian mysticism in our day, has repeatedly defined Christian mysticism in terms of an awareness or encounter with *the presence of God*. The title of his magisterial multi-volume study of the Christian mystical tradition is illustrative of this: *The Presence of God: A History of Western Christian Mysticism*. In fact, the first volume on the foundations of the Christian mystical tradition begins with his treatment of the Old and New Testaments. The consistent thematic thread he identifies throughout the tradition are the ideas of *presence, encounter,* and *transformation*. This corroborates the much more cursory findings we see in what has been uncovered here in our biblical survey.

The mystical element of religion is not something Israel threw off as she began to distinguish herself from the theological systems of her neighbors. What was so radically different about Israel's god was that her god, Yahweh, came to be understood as the God above all gods and, thereby, emphasized Yahweh's all-pervasive presence. This God, the creator of all that is, is a God whose singular desire is to share communion with those made in the divine image and likeness. The whole biblical tradition attests that God will go to whatever lengths to make provision that this communion remain possible; first through the covenantal bonds, then, through the sacrificial system of restitution, and, finally, through the death and resurrection of Jesus Christ. The pervading motive all along was the divine overflow of glory which effects in creation, especially humankind, a transformation or augmentation of nature in order to participate in divine life. Biblically speaking, this participation in the divine nature (cf. 2 Pet 1:4), is the goal of Christian life and the hope of God for the world. This forms the impregnable foundation on which the mystical dimension of the church will blossom in the upcoming two millennia.

THE MYSTICAL DIMENSION IN CHURCH HISTORY

The post-biblical Christian mystical tradition is most often traced back to the towering Origen (185–254), whose commentary on The Song of Songs awakened the Christian consciousness to the possibilities of this book's allegorical application and benefit for the spiritual life and paves a broad avenue on which many would follow and expound. In the Western church, Augustine of Hippo (354–430) would add great depth to this mystical impulse with his *Confessions* and scriptural commentaries. Origen saw the presence of God in all things, especially in Sacred Scripture. This presence was preeminently encountered through the prayerful meditation of the sacred text. The same can be said of Augustine, but Augustine also emphasized the going inward to find God within one's own trinitarian self (memory, knowledge, and love) made in God's image and likeness. In the Eastern church, and contemporaries with Augustine in the west, were the Cappadocians who loomed large and gave the mystical dimension of the church in the east its justifiable foundation. This is most especially true of St. Gregory of Nyssa (335–395). Since Origen and Augustine have already been utilized as paradigm setters for other dimensions, let us now turn to the mystical vision of one of the great luminaries of the east.

St. Gregory of Nyssa

The early years of Gregory's pastoral and writing activity were engulfed in hashing out the theological controversies of his day and his thought bears, in line with this preoccupation, a more intellectual than mystical bent. A significant redirection occurs, however, in the mid 380s when Gregory turns his attention more directly to the life of the spirit and produces the two works which express his mystical vision, each with striking originality. They are his *Commentary on the Canticle of Canticles* and *The Life of Moses*. Werner Jaeger suggests that Gregory's intention at this point in his life was to give a mystical orientation of the monastic way of life begun by his brother Basil.[2] Whatever his impulse, as will be seen, his mystical vision highlights some of the very same themes promoted by our biblical writers with which it bears a notable correspondence, even while expounding with insightful originality.

2. Jeager, *Two Rediscovered Works of Ancient Christian Literature: Gregory of Nyssa and Macarius*, 133–42.

Several characteristics of Gregory of Nyssa's mystical vision stand out as definitive of his work. First is his emphasis on humankind's being created in God's image and likeness. Unlike others in the tradition, Gregory makes no distinction between *image* and *likeness*, whose reality has not been destroyed by sin. Rather, by turning away from God, the human body was deprived of immortality and covered in the *garment of skin*.[3] This *garment of skin* does not prohibit the sinful human person from turning back to God. On the contrary, it causes the human person "to experience a disgust with the things of the world"[4] and incites a desire for its original purity.

A second characteristic of Gregory's mystical vision is the theme of light and darkness. Using Moses as a paradigmatic figure, Gregory demonstrates the spiritual life as moving from light to darkness. The purification of the soul and the restoration of the image and likeness occurs only as the external senses, with its volatile passions, are quieted and the soul's inner life is enlivened through recollection. A true knowledge of God results in the purified soul, and the presence of God is experienced through the grace of contemplation. Jean Daniélou grounds Gregory's mysticism in the Pauline concept of mystery: "it is God's hidden design, which cannot be known without revelation, but can be understood once it is revealed."[5]

A third characteristic is the way Gregory grounds his mystical vision in love, particularly, in love's ecstatic fulfillment of the soul's longing for the Transcendent. Using The Song of Songs as a biblical allegory for the soul's movement into God, Gregory sees the beauty of God as a divine lure drawing the soul out of itself in total dispossession and into the fullness of the Transcendent blessedness. Daniélous notes that Gregory moves beyond the more intellectualistic approaches of Origen and Evagrius and draws a tighter correspondence between knowledge and love where "knowledge becomes love."[6]

This movement of the soul in ecstatic love, for Gregory, leads to a final characteristic of his mystical vision: the eternal progress of the soul. At the heart of this characteristic is a paradox: the soul both draws from the depths of a well and flows in the constant current of a river. From the

---

3. Daniélou, *From Glory to Glory: Texts from Gregory of Nyssa's Mystical Writings*, 12. The phrase *garment of skin* comes from Genesis 3:21 and, according to Daniélou, "is made up of all things which we have in common with animals."

4. Daniélou, *From Glory to Glory: Texts from Gregory of Nyssa's Mystical Writings*, 13.

5. Daniélou, *From Glory to Glory: Texts from Gregory of Nyssa's Mystical Writings*, 28.

6. Daniélou, *From Glory to Glory: Texts from Gregory of Nyssa's Mystical Writings*, 46.

well, the soul lives in peace and stillness. From the river, the soul moves ever in and ever onward. This paradox which lies at the heart of Gregory's thought is captured aptly by Daniélou: "Mystical knowledge is thus always a mixture of knowledge and ignorance, possession and quest, immanence and Transcendence—it is a 'luminous Darkness.'"[7] Yet, even within this paradoxical balance, Gregory does place emphasis on eschatology, giving the future a special power within the soul increased and expanded ever more in its participation in God. Of this, Daniélou writes, "grace endlessly creates ever new eyes to look upon ever new suns."[8]

Pseudo-Dionysius

Although self-purported to be a convert of St. Paul, from The Acts of the Apostles (17:34), this anonymous mystic likely wrote in the late fifth and early sixth centuries. His four extant treatises and ten letters have had a profound influence upon Christian theology and shared no little part in shaping the contours of the Christian mystical tradition. His most important treatise, *The Mystical Theology*, moved Gregory of Nyssa's carefully balanced "luminous Darkness" paradoxicality into a more daring theology of negation and apophaticism. For Dionysius, God is hinted at in the world of image and kataphatic knowledge but only truly known in the darkness beyond what can be conceived by the human mind. If God is goodness, God is a goodness far beyond what the mind can imagine goodness to ever be. Yet, for Dionysius, the work of the mind is crucial to the true knowledge of God in the apophatic experience. Apophaticism needs and depends upon kataphaticism. Nevertheless, the essence of realities cannot be experienced and known purely on the intellectual plain. The intellect bows down before the mystery which the symbol of the words and images contain and leaves the heart to dwell in wonder at the truth encountered therein.

For Dionysius, negation is not to be confused with privation. When Dionysius posits that God is not this or that quality we might normally deem characteristic of the divine, he doesn't mean to say that God is deprived of such qualities but that God is infinitely more than such qualities. Thus, Dionysius negates only to affirm; he negates with the mind to affirm with the heart.

---

7. Daniélou, *From Glory to Glory: Texts from Gregory of Nyssa's Mystical Writings*, 56.
8. Daniélou, *From Glory to Glory: Texts from Gregory of Nyssa's Mystical Writings*, 64.

This process of denial leads logically, experientially, and existentially to silence and turns the interrogation of God by an inquiring human mind into the interrogation of the human heart by an overwhelming divine love. Vulnerable and exposed, the soul can now be fully encompassed by the divine presence of "the brilliant darkness of a hidden silence."[9]

St. Bernard of Clairvaux

St. Bernard of Clairvaux (1090–1153) was a towering figure in the Christendom of the Middle Ages whose charismatic leadership helped transform a struggling "new monastery" into the burgeoning and highly influential Cistercian movement. A foundational part of Bernard's appeal was undoubtedly his spiritual vitality and his ability to articulate in a convincing and instructive way his intimate relationship with God.

Bernard's mysticism, while drawing from the tradition thus far discussed, especially in his love for The Song of Songs, is of a noticeably different tone. In him we hear less of the philosophical and Platonic jargon that nurtured the experience of God in apophatic darkness and more of the biblical imagery of union through encounter modeled in two primary sources: The Song of Songs and in the humanity of Christ fully surrendered to God on the cross. His is a mysticism of experience and loving intimacy.

The starting point of Bernard's mysticism is facing the reality that the human soul is lost and deprived of the presence of God and needs to humble itself in order to begin its return to the experience of love. The ascetical life, then, is a non-negotiable in the spiritual life and always precedes mystical experience. Bernard makes it clear that this is no easy task and will be a struggle, hence the need for a supportive community of like-minded ascetics and contemplatives (Bernard was writing mainly to his fellow monastics). Pride is the main obstacle along the way to a life lived in love and, thus, Bernard's mysticism places special emphasis on the authenticity of expression that humility brings. God is the enemy of pomp and ostentation and the friend of simplicity and truthfulness.

Bernard's mysticism also places great emphasis on the affective component of the spiritual life which results from a life divested of the weight of the love of the things of this world and turned wholly to God. Particularly in his use of The Song of Songs, Bernard had a way of inciting the desire for God in his monks and showing that monastic spirituality need not be

---

9. *Pseudo-Dionysius: The Complete Works*, 135.

only drudgery and gloom but, more properly, delight and wonder. For Bernard, to desire God was, in part, to already possess God. The feeling of the absence of the Bridegroom was, for the person of faith, the assurance of the Bridegroom's return . . . and a new consummation.

The first phrase of The Song of Songs captivated Bernard and offered him an image through which he could work out his mysticism. Several of his first sermons deal with it directly and it is referenced throughout his body of work. It is, "Let him kiss me with the kisses of his mouth" (NABRE, Song of Songs 1:1a). The intimate encounter which "the kiss" symbolizes speaks of the sharing of the sanctified soul with the divine and all the ecstasy that this sharing entails. The symbol also connotes the sustained peace and contemplation which the soul experiences when given the grace to receive this kiss. Knowledge of God results, not from the Bride's intellect thinking about what it would be like to kiss the Bridegroom but from the actual experience of the kissing itself.

The kiss, of course, is symbolic of a spiritual encounter. The Spirit is received in the kiss, and the human heart is filled with divine love and blessing. The Spirit is not manifested in visions or other supernatural manifestations but in the fruits born from the inner life where Spirit has taken residence. Nothing is spoken other than the Eternal Word of Christ, particularly, the crucified Christ, who takes the soul into himself through the kiss of the Spirit and gives to the soul peace and ecstatic joy.

Hildegard of Bingen and The Beguines

A contemporary of St. Bernard of Clairvaux, St. Hildegard of Bingen (1098–1179) was one of the most formidable female figures the church has ever produced. She was one of astonishing talents, integrating within herself multiple vocations: prophet; mystic; composer; dramatist; medical writer; visionary; reformer. She also combines within herself vocations to prayer and contemplation as a Benedictine nun with courageous apostolic activity outside her monastery (something unheard of for a female nun of her time period). In Hildegard we encounter solitude and prayer fervently overflowing into pastoral service and evangelical witness, much like the missionary monks of a previous era. Her contemplative awareness which developed over the numerous years living as a nun (she lived in the care of a nun since she was eight-years-old before becoming a nun herself) helped form an intuitive awareness of all reality and opened her up to the scientific knowledge she developed for her ministry to the sick. Her visions were written down (in both word and illustration) in order to teach others "to know the ways of the Lord" (a literal translation of her major work *Scivias*).

Hildegard, in concert with St. Bernard, gave expression to the feminine aspects of the spiritual life in her emphasis on the Virgin Mary's role in reversing Eve's transgression. Woman is a symbol of the maternal earth from which all life germinates, just as the Virgin Mary will be the maternal earth transfigured by the overshadowing power of the Holy Spirit who will germinate forth the Incarnate Word. This observation leads Hildgegard to conceive of the love of God as a maternal love—a life-giving seed which is nurtured in the soil of the human heart with gentleness and mercy.

Her visions also demonstrate a cosmic perspective where the entire created cosmos is integrated into the life of the Trinitarian God. The four elements of creation are frequently used as sacramental representations of aspects of the divine. In reading Hildegard, one acutely senses the utter accessibility of God and the holiness of each of life's moments and their possibility to surprise and overwhelm.

The thirteenth century was a remarkable century for Christian mysticism, producing such notable mystics as Beatrice of Nazareth (1200–1268), Mechtild of Magdeburg (1210–1285 or 1295), Bonaventure (1221–1274), Raymond Lull (1232–1315), Angela of Foligno (1248–1309), Gertrude the Great (1256–1302), Meister Eckhart (1260–1328), and Marguerite Porete (d. 1310). Three of these mystics were a part of the female lay movement located predominantly in the low countries, known as the Beguines (Beatrice, Mechtild, and Marguerite). These, along with Hadewijch of Antwerp (1150–1200) of the previous century, form the pinnacle of the movement and attest to the power and spiritual fecundity of these remarkable women.

The Beguines were not nuns in the traditional sense. They did not take vows and were not enclosed in a cloister, even if their lifestyle did reflect many of the habits characteristic of the monastic way of life—like voluntary poverty, chastity, and living from the work of their own hands. They developed a spirituality that placed them both in and apart from the world. Living together in common in their beguinage and sharing a life of prayer and worship there, they also served in hospitals and schools. They were at once intensely mystical in their spiritual orientation and intensely generous in their service. The freedom they enjoyed from ecclesiastical control allowed them to develop a form of life that allowed for greater integration of the vertical and horizontal poles of the Christian life. Love for God and love for neighbor inhabited each other in a seamless, symbiotic manner. Such an integration would serve as a model for female religious in the centuries to come as women began to enjoy increasing freedoms to form patterns of life other than one entirely enclosed within the cloister walls.

The mysticism of the Beguines shares many elements in continuity with the traditional monastic spirituality which preceded them. Emphasis on the desert experience of trials, persecution and suffering, as well as on the bridal love imagery so pronounced in Bernard of Clairvaux, marks their general approach to God. Some of the most remarkable writing in this regard was produced by Hadewijch of Antwerp:

> And that kiss will be with one single mouth,
> And to fathom the one single ground,
> And with a single gaze to understand all
> That is, and was, and shall be.[10]

Marguerite Porete was more daring in her mystical vision and was burnt at the stake because of it. The danger of the mystics has always been the blurring of the line between human and divine. This line is all the more blurred when mystics employ poetic imagery in order to convey their experience, which is often employed to express the inexpressible. Drawing inspiration from St. John the Evangelist's identification of God as love, Marguerite expresses the union of God, Love, and Soul with little distinction:

> I am God, says Love, for Love is God and God is Love, and this Soul is God by the condition of Love. I am God by divine nature and this Soul is God by righteousness of Love. Thus this precious beloved of mine is taught and guided by me, without herself, for she is transformed into me, and such a perfect one, says Love, takes my nourishment.[11]

The context in which Marguerite writes is a dialogue between Reason and Love in which Love (and Marguerite) tries to convince Reason that the Soul who has passed through the Virtues belongs no longer to Virtue or herself but entirely to Love. This annihilation of the soul taking leave of the virtues was the main argument the Inquisition brought against her and would be the main concern of the ecclesiastical authorities concerning the mystics and mystical movements in the upcoming centuries. Marguerite

---

10. Cited in Murk-Jansen, *Brides in the Desert: The Spirituality of the Beguines*, 74.
11. *Marguerite Porete: The Mirror of Simple Souls*, 104.

was insistent, however, that it was only in going through the passageway of Virtue that the Soul can arrive at a state of being entirely engulfed in Love.

Quietism

The mystical world which Marguerite Porete opened up with her descriptions of the Soul entirely annihilated with no other motivation but Love (where any motivation at all is a reflection of a lesser state where the Soul's desire, even for good, is implicated by self-interest and, therefore, not at full union with God) would in the centuries to come lead directly to the Quietist controversy of the seventeenth century in the writings of the Spaniard Miguel de Molinos (1628–1696), and the French writings of Jeanne-Marie Bouvier de la Motte (Mme Guyon: 1648–1717) and the Archbishop of Cambrai, François de Salignac de la Motte Fénelon (1651–1715).

Perhaps borrowed from the "prayer of quiet" of St. Teresa of Avila, the so-called Quietism of Molinos, Guyon, and Fénelon was problematic to ecclesial authorities for two main reasons: it was viewed as an extreme form of the mysticism that was very difficult to pastorally control; it was viewed as theologically suspect, being a perversion of the proper relationship between human and divine where the human dimension is "annihilated" by the divine. This second problem is reflected in Molinos' doubt he cast on the salvific role of Christ's mediation in sacraments, meditation, and in human agency in general. It is reflected in Mme Guyon's teaching of the soul's extreme passivity in relation to God and frequently ambiguous views of the distinct mediatorial role of Christ at the soul's summit of union with God. It is reflected in Fénelon's emphasis on a "pure love" that leaves the soul "disinterested" in anything other than the presence of God (hypothetically, even if one were in hell).

Whether the teachings of any of these three writers were ultimately heretical is up for debate. Their efforts to articulate the mystery of the soul's intimate bond with God has helped countless faithful Christians to better understand the possibilities of union with God and has inspired them to seek this union above all other pursuits. What each highlights, though, are the problems that begin to arise when the mystical dimension of ecclesial spirituality becomes relegated almost entirely to the personal. Without being rooted in the other dimensions of ecclesial life, the mystical dimension has a tendency to spiral into extreme forms of individuality and self-transcendence often masking a proclivity for escapism, even if one is seeking to escape into God. The horizontal dimension of Christian life is sacrificed for the vertical and incarnation and cross become subservient to resurrection and glorification. If the mystic's goal is perfection of the soul and union with God, it is never a perfection or union or a God that doesn't lovingly embrace and include all of creation together. Personal intimacy with God and communal fellowship always coincide in Christian spirituality. Even in the privacy of the sanctuary of one's heart is found the mystery of the communion of saints. Seen in this light, a state of total passivity and annihilation devoid of personal motivation is foreign to Christian revelation. There is nothing beyond the divine/human relationship. It is here in the intimate bond between the two that God chose to be glorified. In the words of St. Irenaeus, "The glory of God is the human person fully alive," not fully annihilated.

Thomas Merton

The life of the twentieth century Trappist monk of the Abbey of Gethsemani in rural Kentucky, Thomas Merton (1915–1968), can be studied as a life lived toward greater and greater integration. It may strike one as paradoxical (and Merton was full of paradoxes) to speak of a monk as a person of integration, since, on the surface, it would seem that monastic life is inherently non-integral, rejecting much of human existence that goes into making one fully human, or, in the eyes of some, even fully Christian. Yet, in spite of this popular view of monasticism as isolationist and harmfully ascetical, it can be persuasively argued that it was the particular orientation of monastic life as a life set apart and ordered toward God that allowed Merton to blossom into the man of integration that he would become.

The young Merton who entered the Abbey of Gethsemani in 1941 at twenty-six years of age shared much of the popular ideas about monasticism that a young, idealist ready to turn one's back on the world would share. Merton was very much a man of the world until his conversion to Roman Catholicism in 1938. Having lost both of his parents by the time he was sixteen, Merton would live a rather dissolute life for a time, especially during his brief stint at Cambridge University, as he tried to find his place in the world. Gifted with caring and wise guides at Columbia University where he matriculated, Merton would be led on a healthier path that would eventually lead him to the life-altering experience he had during his first visit to the Abbey of Gethsemani during a Holy Week retreat in 1941.

The weight of God's presence so palpable in the silence of the monastery awakened dimensions within him that mediated a call that was, from his perspective, non-negotiable. He would often describe his experience of God in solitude as a way of finding himself . . . his "true self," as he would refer to it.

After spending twenty-six years living the monastic way of life of prayer, work, and deep reading almost entirely within the enclosure of his monastic walls . . . and after becoming a rather famous monk due to his popular spiritual literary output . . . Merton would have an encounter with God . . . and with humankind . . . that would alter the way he understood himself as a monk. It occurred on the corner of Fourth and Walnut in downtown Louisville on his way to a doctor's visit for his ailing back.

> In Louisville, at the corner of Fourth and Walnut, in the center of the shopping district, I was suddenly overwhelmed with the realization that I loved all those people, that they were mine and I theirs, that we could not be alien to one another even though we were total strangers. It was like waking from a dream of separateness, of spurious self-isolation in a special world, the world of renunciation and supposed holiness . . . .
> This changes nothing in the sense and value of my solitude, for it is in fact the function of solitude to make one realize such things with a clarity that would be impossible to anyone completely immersed in the other cares, the other illusions, and all the automatisms of a tightly collective existence. My solitude, however, is not my own, for I see now how much it belongs to them — and that I have a responsibility for it in their regard, not just in my own. It is because I am one with them that I owe it to them to be alone, and when I am alone, they are not "they" but my own self. There are no strangers![12]

Merton's reconciliation with the world would open up many avenues of bridge-building in the upcoming years that would perdure until his untimely death in 1968, ten years later. Two relationships, in particular, highlight his integral expansion: his relationship to issues of social justice and his ecumenical and inter-religious relationships.

Already having a very powerful pen, Merton began to put it to prophetic use in his writings on pertinent issues facing both the church and the world at large. He addressed racial injustices, issues of peace and non-violence, and was especially concerned about the proliferation of atomic

---

12. Merton, *Conjectures of a Guilty Bystander*, 156–58.

armaments. Many of Merton's readers who received so much from his spiritual books were unsure of what to make of this new orientation, and he was eventually censured by the authorities of his own Cistercian order and not allowed to publish on these issues, them citing that this was the prerogative of bishops, not monks. Merton responded that he was addressing these issues because the bishops weren't.

His bridge-building efforts caused controversy also in his dialogue with Protestants and non-Chrsitians. A small cinder block building was constructed on the monastery grounds so that he could meet with Protestant guests coming to the monastery to learn about the monastic tradition (it would later become his hermitage). Merton was eager to learn from them as well. He began correspondence with several leaders of various religious traditions and was particularly interested in dialogue with monastic forms of life in these traditions, especially Zen Buddhism. One of the great paradoxes of Merton's life was that he left this world near Bangkok while attending a conference on perspectives of inter-monastic life, an ironic, though apt, way of ending a life so committed to realizing integral wholeness.

TOWARD AND INTEGRAL MYSTICAL ECCLESIAL SHAPE

The mystical dimension of ecclesial spirituality is the beating heart of the church. It is the church at prayer and at peace. It is the dimension of the church that enjoys what God has already accomplished for her and rests in the contemplative solitude of this eschatological gift. It is the church which already tastes heaven, already experiences God's saving power, already knows God's eternal embrace. It is the dimension of the church that is utterly convinced by faith that God's work is already finished and only needs to be realized and awakened to. It is the church that enjoys deep intimacy with God and constantly seeks to grow in this intimacy. It is the church that is awake to the presence of God in all of creation and seeks to awaken to it more and more. It is the church that embraces traditional forms of asceticism and any discipline that would help her militate against anything that would impede her enjoyment of God and her further growth into God.

The mystics of Sacred Scripture and church history witness to the possibilities that are available to us as humans through the power of grace. They attest to the highest potentialities of human experience and demonstrate that these potentialities are realized only in relationship to the divine. They help the church always remember that Christian life is always fundamentally about a relationship, the human with the divine, and serve as a constant reminder of what an awesome privilege it is to be chosen by God.

Working in tandem with the intellectual dimension which places emphasis on the mind, the mystical dimension places emphasis on the heart. The heart has always been considered the most sacred of realities, both in God and in humans, and is the place where all dimensions converge. The four previous dimensions discussed (evangelical, pentecostal, sacramental, and intellectual) lead toward it and the two following dimensions (pastoral and prophetic) flow from it. Without the mystical dimension of prayer, contemplation, and the enjoyment of God's presence, the church loses its heart and struggles to maintain its vibrancy and its *raison d'etre*, which is communion with God. All manner of dysfunction results.

Without the mystical dimension, the evangelical dimension preaches to win souls for a cause but not for God, the pentecostal dimension gets stuck in emotionalism and never learns to discover the silent center which the emotions are meant to open up, the sacramental dimension becomes fixated on ritualism and rubrics and the grace being mediated by them is aborted from reaching the soil of the heart, the intellectual dimension gets stuck in the mind and never lets the knowledge of the truth sink into the heart and become transformational, the pastoral dimension becomes work instead of a way of encountering Christ in those being served, the prophetic dimension slips into offering little more than angry and frustrated denunciations and loses the position for insight that solitude brings. But with the mystical dimension nurtured and fully alive, the vitality of the other dimensions is assured, being rooted in the generating source by which each can reach its effective end.

CHAPTER 6

A Church of Charitable Concern

The Pastoral Dimension

SCRIPTURAL ROOTS

"Yahweh is my shepherd, I lack nothing" (NJB, Ps 23:1) sums up Israel's understanding of God's paternal role over her. Yahweh, often in striking contradistinction to the foreign gods of Israel's neighboring nations, was fundamentally a compassionate and caring divine being, though quite capable of wrath and fierce retribution. Nevertheless, Israel always held out the hope and conviction that Yahweh's heart was most fundamentally one full of loving mercy and responded in wrath only when provoked by human sinfulness. So she could cry, ". . . in wrath remember mercy" (NJB, Hab 3:2c).

The most perduring and resonate image of this faithful love of Yahweh was captured in the image of the shepherd guiding and caring for his sheep, effectively exploited throughout the Psalms and Prophets and personified in those Yahweh called to be his representatives: Abraham; Moses; Joshua; Samuel; David, to name a few of the most significant. Ezekiel would prophesy about the gross failure of Israel's leaders to fulfill this role and condemn those who shepherd themselves rather than Yahweh's flock.[1]

The prophets, whose vocation was to condemn sin and give voice to Yahweh's wrath, are often, notably, also eager to express Yahweh's loving kindness: "I have loved you with an everlasting love and so I still maintain my faithful love for you" (NJB, Jer 31:3). In Hosea, the faithful love of

---

1. See Ezekiel 34 for the prophet's vision of good and bad shepherding.

Yahweh is most striking. Even though Yahweh is spurned by Israel, he says, "I shall cure them of their disloyalty, I shall love them with all my heart" (NJB, Hos 14:4). Second Isaiah, the most developed section in all of the prophetic literature on the theme of Yahweh's loving kindness, expresses the heart of Yahweh thus: "Since I regard you as precious, since you are honored and I love you, . . . do not be afraid, for I am with you" (NJB, Is 43:4–5).

Associated with Yahweh's faithful love revealed in the image of the shepherd are other images which highlight not only Yahweh's love but also Yahweh's mercy (Ps 136; Isa 54:10), Yahweh's compassion (Ps 145:9), and Yahweh's delight (Ps 35:27). The Old Testament, thus, abounds with imagery attesting to the compassionate care that Yahweh shows toward those called by his name.

Standing in direct continuity with the witness of the Old Testament about Yahweh as Shepherd, is the New Testament witness of Jesus Christ as the Good Shepherd. Christ, for the Gospel writers, especially John, definitively reveals the heart of God and does so primarily through the image of the shepherd guarding and caring for his sheep. What is particular and most revelatory about the Johannine Good Shepherd, though, is the extent of his care and compassion: he lays down his life for the sheep (John 10:11, 15) and promises eternal life to those who hear his voice and follow him (John 10:10).

Those so called, the community of disciples or the church, are, in turn, to take up the role of shepherd and engage in the care and compassion of its members, as well as of those outside the fold. Certain members are especially appointed for this task, as we see in the office of deacon, of presbyter, and of bishop.[2] The function of these pastoral leaders, as articulated in the New Testament, went beyond the care and compassion of the flock. It also included teaching, administration, discernment, and correction. Yet, at the heart of the church's pastoral ministry was the special care and attention given to the poor, the oppressed, and the most vulnerable of society (i.e. widow and orphan).

Jesus, like Ezekiel, was acutely concerned with pastoral leaders who pastured themselves off on their sheep. Some of Jesus' most vitriolic statements are aimed at the religious leaders of Israel who did, in his view, just

---

2. These are the primary terms used in the NT to describe the pastoral leadership in the early church. The NT itself attests to the overlap of meaning in these terms. A distinct three-fold hierarchy would develop only in the second century.

that. What was most disconcerting for Jesus was the neglect of Israel's most vulnerable by the shepherds who were more concerned with their own profiteering and religious/social status. In stark contrast, Jesus embodied humility, the divestment of both religious and social ambition, and sought to come to the aid of the most vulnerable—and not only of Israel but also of the unclean pagans.

The Acts of the Apostles demonstrates, in mirror image, Jesus' ministry in the ministry of Peter and Paul, the two main representatives of the church in this early testament of Christian faith. The author of Acts was quite intent on demonstrating that Jesus continues his pastoral ministry through the church acting in his name. Besides the apostolic ministry of preaching and teaching, Peter and Paul engaged in the pastoral ministry of healing. Preaching the gospel, explicating it in teaching, and communicating its power in healing were three aspects of one act of redemption . . . God saving, making whole, and establishing the Kingdom of Heaven on earth. The commission of the Twelve is just that: "Cure the sick, raise the dead, cleanse those suffering from virulent skin-diseases, drive out devils. You received without charge, give without charge" (NJB, Matt 10:8).

DEFINING CHARACTERISTICS

Perhaps out of all the dimensions of the church, the pastoral dimension is the most self-evident. Since it consists of the outward display of care and compassion, it is either present or not and can be verified through its concrete expression. The contours of charitable service that are revealed by our survey of both Old and New Testaments, thus, are the following:

- *Shepherd imagery* is one of the most significant images for Israel's god, Yahweh.
- Yahweh is *moved with compassion* for Israel and for the oppressed of the earth.
- Yahweh is *more defined by love than by wrath.*
- Yahweh's love reveals itself in other closely related features: *mercy; compassion; delight.*
- Yahweh has a particular interest in the *well-being of Israel* and in *protecting her from harm.*
- *Jesus Christ is depicted as embodying* the loving concern of Yahweh.

- The extent of Yahweh's loving concern is revealed in Christ as *without limit* and to the end, the sacrifice of one's life.
- The New Testament gives special emphasis to Jesus' care for the *poor and oppressed*.
- Special concern is also given to the *foreigner*, the non-Israelite.
- The prophetic literature and Jesus, in line with the prophets, *articulate very harsh condemnations* toward religious leaders who fail in their pastoral responsibilities.
- Jesus *commissioned leaders* among his followers to carry on his pastoral ministry.
- *Love is the most defining characteristic of the Christian community*, holding more weight of significance than any other.
- *Love is also the most defining characteristic of God*, explicitly stated in 1 John and implicitly demonstrated throughout Sacred Scripture.

THE PASTORAL DIMENSION IN CHURCH HISTORY

Pastoral care in the church followed the pattern of the New Testament, focusing on the defined characteristics above and developing an institutional structure that would support and accommodate it into the future and in various circumstances. Yet, these basic pastoral concerns addressed the issues of a persecuted community often struggling with needs unique to their situation, yet, while also struggling with the needs that are common to any community, like tending to the poor, caring for the sick, supporting the socially outcast, and providing sacramental ministry. A seismic shift occurred, however, in the fourth century that would pose acute challenges to the way pastoral care in the church was exercised.

The conversion of Constantine in the early fourth century decisively changed the membership of the church from one of a persecuted minority whose faith was quite intentional to an accepted body of converts. This pastoral situation would help fuel the spread of monastic communities whose members longed for the original fervor of a community on the margins and would move the church toward forming two major models of discipleship: the monastery and the parish (i.e. lay community). The lines between the two models came to be blurred, however, when many of the monastic ascetics became bishops. The spiritual wisdom of the cloister began to be translated in an applicable way for the church at large. It was at this time that the pastoral treatise took definite shape and provided for the needs of a church facing the new pastoral situation of a post-Constantinian reality. Several notable figures contributed: St. Gregory Nazianzus; St. Ambrose of Milan; St. John Chrysostom, to name three of the most notable. The most influential, however, was to be the treatise of the monk/bishop (and pope) St. Gregory the Great (540–604), his *Liber regulae pastoralis* or *Book of Pastoral Rule*.

St. Gregory the Great

Combining both the monastic and ecclesiastic worlds in himself, Gregory was uniquely poised to speak effectively to both community models and shepherd both monastery and diocese. Shortly after beginning his pontificate, he sent, in 590, his pastoral treatise to John, archbishop of Ravenna. In it, Gregory identifies the traits of an authentic shepherd and cautions against allowing just anyone to lead the flock of God. He writes of the priest's daily tasks and offers advice about the many pastoral challenges that they will inevitably face.

Gregory begins his treatise by noting that "No one presumes to teach an art that he has not first mastered through study. How foolish it is therefore for the inexperienced to assume pastoral authority when the care of souls is the art of arts."[3] The ideal pastoral leader, for Gregory, is the experienced ascetic who has acquired the wisdom that comes from spending years in prayer and the engagement of the spiritual disciplines. For this reason, he was adamant about guarding against unworthy candidates from assuming pastoral leadership and about encouraging gifted ascetics in taking on pastoral roles. Ideally, it was the one who combined a deep contemplative life with an acute pastoral sense who made the most qualified candidate for pastoral leadership.

Apart from the ascetic discipline of celibacy, Ambrose and Augustine did not lay heavy emphasis on the other aspects of the spiritual disciplines to be developed in priests. Gregory, however, would envision the pastoral leader more in line with the ascetic spiritual father and encourage a priesthood that takes special interest in the spiritual well-being of the lay congregation. The tradition of monastic spiritual direction, therefore, began to make a direct impact on pastoral leadership in the wider church.

3. Gregory the Great, *The Book of Pastoral Rule*, 27.

In line with Benedict of Nursia, who was a great inspiration to Gregory, discretion would also comprise an important component to effective pastoral ministry. There were moments when the spiritual father should relax particular discipline for the sake of charity and the encouragement of spiritual growth. Yet, there were also times when the spiritual father should assert his authority and deal out the required measure of justice. Discretion was the spiritual gift that allowed for the proper administration of each in their proper accord. Pastoral flexibility is the art learned only through one's own authentic spiritual engagement with God.

Gregory's method of pastoral ministry also took into consideration the unique, individual circumstances of those receiving pastoral care. The goal was always the employment of the most effective remedy to heal, restore, and rehabilitate the person or community in need. Pastoral ministry was always to be personalized and never generic and routine. The longest section of the treatise is devoted to identifying exemplary pastoral traits and their opposites so as to encourage good pastoral practice. For example, one who is committed to lifelong celibacy should be cared for differently from one who is not. One who is seemingly demonstrating patience can possibly be actually exhibiting resentment. No one in the patristic era matches Gregory for his psychological profiling and pastoral insights.

Gregory's teaching was substantiated by his many pastoral initiatives as Pope. Most notable was his commitment in promoting almsgiving among the faithful, especially in Rome. He developed an extensive relief system that brought aid to the poor, many of whom were refugees from the raids of the Lombards. For Gregory, the wealth of the church belonged to the poor, the church being only wealth's stewards. The administrative genius of Gregory, combined with his clearly evident pastoral sense, not only made him a highly effective pastoral leader but also caused him to be much beloved by the faithful of Rome and beyond.

John Wyclif

It is commonly acknowledged that the great ecclesial paradigm shift that occurred in the church in the sixteenth century, otherwise known as the Protestant Reformation, followed by the Roman Catholic Counter-Reformation, finds its beginnings in reform-minded clerics calling for change centuries before these transformative events. Often cited as one of the most significant early voices of protest was the Englishman, John Wycliffe

(1330–1384), often referred to as "the morning star of the Reformation." Wycliffe's primary concern for church reform was the reform of the clergy who, in his estimation, were largely failing in their pastoral roles. The Black Death was certainly one major circumstantial factor which precipitated the demise of the clergy—both in number and in the ability for the church to adequately form new pastoral leaders. The major pastoral function of the priest, in Wycliffe's judgment, especially in the particular ecclesial crisis of the fourteenth century, was the proper and effective passing on of the true knowledge of Christ and inciting faith in him through the proclamation of the gospel (something the Second Vatican Council would eventually assert in the mid-twentieth century in its decree *Presbyterorum ordinis*). For this reason, Wycliffe was driven to his translation project of the Bible. The main function of the priest was, then, "to point to the Eternal Word from the words written in the Bible . . . to say the same thing as the Bible but in other words, so that the Eternal Word might be heard in multiple ways . . . . To the degree that the pastor speaks in accordance with the Eternal Word, his words will likewise resonate and have the transformative power conveyed by Scripture."[4] In Benjamin L. Fischer's estimation, Wycliffe's reform program had three primary prongs: the conformation of the lives of the preachers to the apostolic model; calling the nobility to both spiritual and civil stewardship; the promotion of theological knowledge in the vernacular to ensure the propagation of sound learning.[5] The first and third points directly involve the role and function of the priest. In addressing these points of urgent concern, Wycliffe, in his writings on pastoral leadership, pronounces numerous condemnations on wayward clergy and their particular shortcomings, and, in turn, offers a portrait of the virtuous pastoral leader.

In the opening section of his treatise, *De officio pastoralis* ("On the Pastoral Office"), Wycliffe states plainly the two main aspects of a good shepherd: "There are two things that fall to the office of the shepherd: holiness of life and sound teaching."[6] He then proceeds to identify a number of characteristics that befit priests who have conformed their lives to Christ:

- Priests must be content (particularly with food and clothing)

---

4. Fischer, *Being a Pastor: Pastoral Treatises of John Wycliffe*, 12.
5. Fischer, *Being a Pastor: Pastoral Treatises of John Wycliffe*, 13–14.
6. Fischer, *Being a Pastor: Pastoral Treatises of John Wycliffe*, 19.

- Priests ought to be the most obedient and act in Christlike simplicity in relation to secular authority
- Priests should give freely of their own possessions
- Priests should prefer to lose their office and suffer death before assenting to ecclesial authority wrongfully administered
- Priests should never withhold tithes or consent to sin
- Priests should reside with their flock and guard against absenteeism
- Priests should guard against false teaching and promote sound teaching
- Priests should live disciplined and exemplary lives

Wycliffe elaborates on the specific functions of the pastor: he is to feed the sheep; he is to protect their sheep from wolves; he is to anoint the wounded sheep and share with them the medicine of God's Word whereby they may be made whole.[7]

In another work on pastoral leadership, Wycliffe becomes more biting in tone and identifies the several illnesses plaguing the clergy of his day:

- Priests commonly live in simony, selling their masses and the sacrament for worldly filth and carnal pleasure
- Priests bring slander and reproach on the holy office by a worldly life and ignorance of the Holy Scriptures
- Priests scandalize people by their example of idleness and indulgence
- Priests occupy themselves overmuch in worldly occupations and secular offices against the commands of Holy Scripture
- Priests often receive considerable payment for they prayers
- Priests are more concerned with erring in the liturgy than with the commands of God
- Priests take a vow of chastity and then seduce women
- Priests often seek worldly honor and acquisition more than the honor of God
- Priests are sometimes like hell, always covetous yet never filled

---

7. Fischer, *Being a Pastor: Pastoral Treatises of John Wycliffe*, 44.

But good priests are those "who live well in holiness of thought, speech, deeds, and example to the people, who teach God's Word according to their knowledge, and who work night and day to learn better and teach clearly and continually, are true prophets and holy messengers of God. They are spiritual lights of the world, as God says by his prophets and by Jesus Christ in the gospel, and saints declare it well by authority and reason."[8]

St. Francis de Sales

If John Wycliffe was referred to as "the morning star of the Reformation," one might be justified in referring to Francis de Sales (1567–1622) as "the evening star of the Counter-Reformation." As about as different in temperament and pastoral sensibilities from Wycliffe as is possible, Francis de Sales, who became the Roman Catholic Bishop in Calvinist Geneva, would exert his pastoral ministry with qualities quite distinct from the fourteenth century Englishman. Wycliffe was a pastor with strong prophetic tendencies. De Sales was a pastor with strong mystical tendencies. Wycliffe was predominantly concerned with the reform of clerical morality. De Sales was predominantly concerned with the reform of clerical (and lay) spirituality. Conformity to Christ was at the center of both programs of reform. Yet, the pastoral approach of Francis de Sales who found himself in a post-Reformation world populated predominantly by Calvinists would ultimately prove so effective because of his docile humility balanced with his zealous preaching that gave strikingly clear and convincing reasons for reforming one's life toward a more devout and holy way.

After struggling with the belief of his eternal damnation in the Calvinistic ambiance of his day, Francis would come to emphasize the all-pervading love of God that casts out fear. His Christianity was a joyful and optimistic one, and his pastoral ministry revealed itself in gentle, yet, fervent labor to win over the hearts of the flock to the all-pervading, divine love of God. With his writings, his influential *Introduction to the Devout Life* and his more specialized masterpiece, *Treatise on the Love of God*, Francis would invite all, not just those in the cloister, to become saints—ultimately inspiring "the universal call to holiness" of the Second Vatican Council. His pastoral concern led him to speak and write in a manner that was digestible to all, articulating the faith less in highly intellectual categories, as was common in his day, and more in simple and direct ways that focused on

---

8. Fischer, *Being a Pastor: Pastoral Treatises of John Wycliffe*, 72.

the cultivation of a particular virtue and the practical life adjustments one needed to make to lead a holier Christian life. It is believed that his effective pastoral ministry brought over forty-thousand converts to Calvinism back to the Roman fold.

One of the greatest contributions of Francis de Sales to the wider church was the Order of the Visitation that he co-founded in 1610 with Jeanne de Chantal. This female religious community, unlike many of the women's orders previously founded up to that point in the church's history, sought to combine a deeply spiritual life of contemplation with the active ministry of caring for the poor and infirm. This model of contemplation and action would eventually inspire many female religious communities in the future to come but was a little too ahead of its time for the seventeenth century. In 1618, the archbishop of Lyons would upset this balance of contemplation and action and force full enclosure on the sisters and alter its original shape.

Mother Teresa

Of the many female religious communities that would model themselves off of the contemplation and action paradigm, the Missionaries of Charity have become one of the most visible and widely respected. St. Teresa of Calcutta (1910–1997), still affectionately referred to as "Mother Teresa," was the foundress and main visionary behind this global order. At the age of 18, Anjezë Gonxhe Bojaxhiu (Teresa's given name) would travel from her native Albania to Ireland where she would enter the Sisters of Loreto, take the name "Teresa," and aspire to become a missionary, being inspired by her patroness, St. Thérèse of Lisieux, the patron saint of missionaries. After teaching in a school in Calcutta for nearly twenty years, Teresa was moved by compassion for the poor of the sprawling Calcutta. She experienced what she described as "a call within a call" and left the relative comfort of her convent to live amidst the poorest of the poor and to help minister to their needs in total solidarity.

In 1950, the Vatican established the Missionaries of Charity as a diocesan congregation which allowed it to fulfill its mission of caring for "the hungry, the naked, the homeless, the crippled, the blind, the lepers, all those people who feel unwanted, unloved, uncared for throughout society, people that have become a burden to the society and are shunned by everyone."[9]

9. Teresa of Calcutta, "Mother Teresa: In Her Own Words."

During the following decade, as the congregation began to grow, it would expand its outreach throughout India opening hospices, orphanages, and leper houses across the country. During the 1970s, it would expand its outreach internationally, founding ministries in dozens of countries throughout Asia, Africa, America, and Europe. Today, the Missionaries of Charity boast over four-thousand five-hundred sisters ministering in over one-hundred thirty countries and consists of both active and contemplative branches, as well as a community of men.

The charitable work of Mother Teresa and the Missionaries of Charity has been nearly universally acknowledged and hallowed, both inter-denominationally throughout the church and internationally. Her arresting, humble pastoral presence has brought her before the most powerful rulers of the world, and her extensive charitable contributions garnered her the Nobel Peace Prize in 1979, "for work undertaken in the struggle to overcome poverty and distress, which also constitutes a threat to peace."[10] Pope Benedict XVI, writing in his first encyclical, *Deus caritas est*, references Mother Teresa repeatedly and uses her as an exemplary model to support one of the main theses of his work: "In the example of Blessed Teresa of Calcutta we have a clear illustration of the fact that time devoted to God in prayer not only does not detract from effective and loving service to our neighbor but is in fact the inexhaustible source of that service."[11]

Pope John XXIII and Pope Francis

The most visible pastoral position of the universal church, the Roman Catholic Bishop of Rome, has been recently occupied by two strikingly pastoral pontiffs who, each in their own way, has reminded both the church herself, and the world beyond, what Christian pastoral leadership looks like. Perhaps the reason why their style of pastoral leadership has been so notably striking is because, in the opinion of many, the leadership in this same church has all too often been exercised less like Christlike shepherds and more like political potentates. Pastoral leadership and authority go hand-in-hand. Even though there have been Christian communities who have tried to eliminate any trace of authority within their polity and pastoral ministries, favoring a more egalitarian manner of ministry, historically, the church has exercised its pastoral ministries in a more hierarchical fashion

---

10. "Nobel Committee: The Nobel Peace Prize 1979 press release."
11. Pope Benedict XVI, *Deus caritas est*.

through ordained representatives who are commissioned for their particular ministries. Being endowed with the authority of Christ and the church, they are sent to minister in Jesus' name. This model, of course, has ample biblical support, even if the exact configuration of these ministries is not always clear. Yet, the misuse of this authority also has biblical precedent. Hence, the desire, for some throughout history, to dispose of authoritative structures altogether.

Within the ecclesial traditions who have retained a hierarchical pastoral structure, though, the Popes of the Roman Catholic Church have had a notorious history. The same church that has produced a St. Gregory the Great has also produced a Pope John XII (937–964) who gave land to a mistress, murdered several people, and was killed by a man who caught him in bed with his wife. The papacy was also occupied by powerful potentates from the likes of Innocent III (1161–1216) to Pius IX (1792–1878) who exploited their authority in order to amass greater ecclesial power for themselves. Especially in the shadow of the carefully diplomatic Pius XII (1876–1958) and the brilliantly intellectual Benedict XVI (1927–2022), John XXIII (1881–1963) and Francis (b. 1936) stand in stark contrast to their immediate predecessors who used their authority to emphasize ecclesial aspects other than the specifically pastoral kind. What caused such sensation in the mid-twentieth century and what has caused such sensation in the past decade is how remarkably pastorally sensitive John XXIII and Francis have been. However varied their pontificates may, in the end, be assessed, little argument will be given to the fact that they were at heart shepherds utilizing their pastoral authority primarily in the service of the good of the lay faithful and the wider world, especially the most vulnerable and needy, and not for the buttressing up of their own, or their institution's, temporal power and prestige. Both were imminently concerned with a church turned in on itself and the incipient clericalism that results from such a disposition. Both understood that the world and the church together, at this time in history, need pastoral leadership that gives emphasis, not primarily to diplomatic maneuvering or to intellectual precision, but to the compassionate care of the flock, within the fold or without; that selflessly gives away its own life in humble service in imitation of the chief shepherd, Jesus Christ.

A CHURCH OF CHARITABLE CONCERN

A Crisis in Pastoral Leadership

Scandal has never been foreign to the life of the church. Beginning with the original apostolic community, within nearly every Pauline church attested to in the New Testament, and within the universal church throughout the centuries, including its various denominational branches, pastoral leaders have consistently shepherded themselves off on their sheep and have misused and abused their pastoral authority. What makes this infringement of pastoral ministry especially egregious and particularly scandalous is the specific nature of Christian pastoral concern embodied in Christ as a leader who consistently placed the good of the other ahead of himself . . . at whatever cost. The Good Shepherd is, above all, an embodiment of sacrificial love. Such a high ideal makes the failures of Christian pastoral leadership all the more obvious and, in turn, condemnatory. What creates scandal is not the general shortcomings of pastors, it is their sinfulness that quite intentionally places their own selfish desires over others, often the others to whom they are charged to serve. It is, fundamentally, a corruption of authority and a duplicity of character where the wolf is dressed in sheep's clothing.

Today, there are two primary manifestations of this corruption in pastoral leadership. The first is in the area of finances. The second is in the area of sexuality. The first has been a symptom found mainly in the evangelical and pentecostal wings of the church. The second has been a symptom found mainly in the Roman Catholic Church. Yet, each, to a certain extent, are problems throughout the church as a whole.

It would be easy to name names in the case of each, since the nature of scandal is the public notoriety of the given events, but the point to be made here has to do with illuminating the true nature of pastoral authority by exposing how it has been corrupted and abused, not the individuals involved. What makes the Christian leader who solicits money from the flock so that he can buy a new, better private jet so scandalous is the carefully crafted rhetoric and highly selective biblical texts used to justify such actions. What makes the faith-healer whose healing ministry preys on the hopes and aspirations of the vulnerable so corrupt is the way Christ's name is invoked in the very process through which the faith-healer amasses obscene amounts of wealth. What makes the priest who sexually abuses children so frighteningly horrific is that one's pastoral authority and position is exploited to maximize the possibility of grooming the vulnerable and then violating human innocence. What makes the cover-up of this gross sin so egregious is that bishops are ordained to protect, defend, and nurture the flock, not expose it further to predatory priests. When protecting the institution of the church from scandal becomes more important than charity and justice for the "little ones," the scandalous events become all the more scandalous. What makes the domineering, mirco-managing pastor who rules like an autocrat so scandalous is the utter lack of Christian humility which prefers to serve rather than be served.

And yet, the crisis in pastoral leadership goes far beyond the scandalous behavior of some pastoral leaders. Today's ecclesial communities throughout the world face a crisis of leadership that extends from the severe lack of shepherds that causes undue stress on those already ordained (along with the hasty ordination of unqualified and unhealthy candidates), to the ideologically motivated leaders who are more interested in promoting their own religious and moral agenda than serving the people of God with care and compassion. Then there is the crisis of credibility that the recent sex scandals, coupled with an increasingly secularized society, have helped create. This complex convergence of forces has, especially in the western world, caused a widespread exodus from active ecclesial life and an equally widespread deafening to the voices coming from Christian pulpits of those who remain. Yet, the discreditation of pastoral leadership aimed mostly at the hypocrisy of Chrsitian leaders who do not do what they preach should not overshadow the often heroic service done by so many exemplary pastors and community outreach programs. There is nothing about acts of love that can be criticized. Perhaps, it is through the inherent integrity of authentic pastoral leadership, most of all, that the credibility of the church can be restored and the gospel can once again be heard and received.

TOWARD AN INTEGRAL PASTORAL ECCLESIAL SHAPE

If Christians are known by their love for one another (John 13:35) and by their sacrificial love for the world (John 3:16) and will be judged by the good deeds they have shown "to the least of these" (Matt 25:40), then it can be said that the pastoral dimension of the church is the surest sign that the church's faith is authentic. The pastoral dimension plays, therefore, an authenticating role in the life of the church and consistently grounds the other dimensions in the life of God through its embodiment of Christ's great commission. As a dimension of ministration, the pastoral dimension (and the prophetic dimension to follow) functions as a revelatory component of the dimensions of initiation and maturation which precede it, communicating the content of the gospel of God through the imitation of Christ in compassionate and selfless service. As such, it manifests the love of God, whose love overflows in the acts of creation, incarnation, and redemption and becomes, in doing so, the healing and reconciling presence of God in the world.

The pastoral dimension is the dimension of charity, of compassion, and of concern. The Spirit which fills the church is a Spirit which moves the church with a dynamic thrust out of itself toward the areas of greatest need in the world. The integration of the life of the church into Christ, which is the work of the Spirit, cannot remain satisfied, content, or comfortable in its dimensions of feeding on the Word of God, of enjoying the power of God's Spirit, of being touched by God's sacramental presence, of growing in the understanding of the mystery of God, or of awakening to the full realization of life with God. All of these experiences of Christian life are preparatory for a life lived in the ecstatic love of God which finds its fulfillment in charitable concern.

While the whole church is called to participate in the loving overflow of life in Christ through the power of the Spirit, pastoral leaders are particularly ordained and commissioned to embody the shepherd's heart to the flock of God. It is crucially important that today's leaders have a clear understanding of their pastoral role in this regard. While the pastor and priest is ordained and commissioned to fulfill several functions in the life of the church, from administrator to preacher to sacramental leader of the community, it is the compassionate concern for the people of God and the most vulnerable of the world that must arrest his or her greatest attention and concern. The gospel the preacher proclaims from the pulpit falls flat and loses a great deal of its power if it doesn't come from a heart seared with the fire of God's compassionate love. For the gospel is not just a message proclaimed in word but in deed and in power (1 Cor 12:28). Or, as the author of 1 John states without equivocation, "Whoever does not love does not know God, for God is love" (NRSVUE, 1 John 4:8).

Therefore, without the pastoral dimension firmly active within the life of the church, the evangelical dimension runs the danger of losing credibility, the pentecostal dimension runs the risk of becoming insular and self-absorbed, the sacramental dimension runs the risk of neglecting the sacramental moments of healing, the intellectual dimension runs the risk of mistaking the ideal for the real, the mystical dimension runs the risk of believing union with God is achieved by a pathway other than love, and the prophetic dimension runs the risk of tearing down without ever rebuilding. But with the pastoral dimension firmly in place, the evangelical dimension can restore its credibility and expand its saving message, the pentecostal dimension can tap into a power that only comes through selfless concern, the sacramental dimension can operate in full capacity offering the most vulnerable a powerful experience of God in their time of need, the intellectual dimension can use its ideals to meet the needs of real life situations, the mystical dimension can flow more fully in the Trinitarian flow of God's love, and the prophetic dimension can prevent itself from missing the true goal of justice, which is always restoration and redemption.

The church must always ask itself if it looks like Christ or not. This is the test of its integrity. Its credibility rests solely upon this reality: whether she is willing to suffer for the sake of the other . . . no matter who that other may be. As suggested above, it may be the only way that her gospel can be heard once again and her image as a community that is known through their love for one another can be restored. To know clearly that the dimensions of initiation and maturation are directed toward the pastoral manifestation of charitable concern can help the church harness the spiritual energy of these dimensions toward their God-given potential and make her witness to Christ all the more transformative.

CHAPTER 7

The Conscience of the Church

The Prophetic Dimension

The word "prophetic" is quite in vogue today and is thrown around to speak about and justify many different kinds of spiritual realities. So, it is important that we are very clear about the particular usage being employed here when we refer to the church as having a prophetic dimension. As we will see, the prophetic function among the ancient Hebrews is already a varied phenomenon. It will continue to be so in the life of the Christian church from its inception until the present day. From the witness of scripture and church history, there are two main components to the "prophetic" that can be discerned. First, there is the act of "forthtelling," by which the prophet speaks forth the Word of the Lord or symbolically acts in such a way as to criticize and challenge a given belief or practice and reveal the truth that comes from God. Secondly, there is the charismatic "foretelling" of what God is about to do sometime in the future. This act is often accompanied by spiritual frenzy and enthusiasm. As a Spirit-inspired charism, it more properly belongs to the pentecostal dimension of the church and will be referred to as such in this chapter. What we are primarily concerned with here is the dimension of the church that bears witness to truth and justice through the "forthtelling" word and symbolic deed in service to both the health and integrity of the church and to the salvation of the world.

THE SHAPE OF THE CHURCH

SCRIPTURAL ROOTS

Prophecy in the Old Testament is often categorized in the terms "former prophets" and "latter prophets." The designation "former prophets" refers to the prophets of the books of Joshua, Judges, 1–2 Samuel, and 1–2 Kings. They would include, among others, Joshua, Samuel, Elijah, and Elisha. "Latter prophets" refers to the prophets of the prophetic literature who have books named in their honor. Among these, the "Major Prophets" would be Isaiah, Jeremiah, and Ezekiel. The "Minor Prophets" would be The Twelve remaining shorter prophetic books. One major problem with this categorization is that neither category contains who, in the tradition, was considered by many as the greatest of the prophetic figures of the Hebrew people: Moses.

Walter Brueggemann, whose justly lauded book *The Prophetic Imagination* did so much to ground the prophetic dimension of the church in solid biblical exegesis and helped the church to understand what is properly prophetic in the biblical sense today, uses Moses as the prophet par excellence in illuminating and demonstrating his thesis. Brueggemann's thesis is discussed in the Preface to the First Edition in what follows:

> The following discussion is an attempt to understand what the prophets were up to, if we can be freed from our usual stereotypes of foretellers or social protesters. Here it is argued that they were concerned with most elemental changes in human society and that they understood a great deal about how change is effected. The prophets understood the possibility of change as linked to emotional extremities of life. They understood the strange incongruence between public conviction and personal yearning. Most of all, they understood the distinctive power of language, the capacity to speak in ways that evoke newness "fresh from the word." It is argued here that a prophetic understanding of reality is based in the notion that all social reality does spring fresh from the word. It is the aim of every totalitarian effort to stop the language of newness, and we are now learning that where such language stops we find our humanness diminished.[1]

Brueggemann argues that Moses' act of liberation through the exodus and the establishment of a new way of being forged through the wilderness journey was an act of an imagination that was creative and free enough to envision an alternative way of being in both the area of religion and

---

1. Brueggemann, *The Prophetic Imagination*, xiii.

politics. In religion, the "static triumphalism" of Egypt's polytheistic system is now being replaced by "Yahweh, the sovereign one who acts in his lordly freedom, is extrapolated from no social reality and is captive to no social perception but acts from his own person toward his own purposes."[2] In politics, the exploitation and oppression of Egypt is now being replaced by "a *politics of justice and compassion*."[3]

Moses' prophetic activity, Brueggemann notes, was marked by the dual function of criticizing and energizing.[4] The function of criticism is to provide an alternative consciousness to the predominant, prevailing consciousness that would move the hearer of the prophetic word to act differently. The function of energizing is to provide an alternative consciousness that would offer models and possibilities for acting differently. It is to offer hope that life can be better and to provide justifiable reasons why this is so. Moses does just this when he criticizes the idolatry of Egypt and begins to articulate the theology of Yahweh. Israel finds freedom precisely by embracing the new consciousness that Yahweh provides. Israel maintains her freedom by living in the covenantal relationship that this new consciousness creates.

In this sense, Moses, the prophet, is a seer. Through his spirit-inspired imagination he sees an alternative future for Israel and is willing to courageously act on their behalf through a faith that daringly believes the Word of God spoken to him. This prophetic role, then, involves discerning the truth of Yahweh's voice in contradistinction to the voices of all the other gods. This discernment then leads to a decision: a yes and a no . . . a for and an against. The prophetic function is a function of decisiveness and decision. It gives little room for equivocation. ". . . choose today whom you will serve" (NABRE, Joshua 24:15).

This Spirit-inspired call to fidelity to the new consciousness that Yahweh provides and the covenantal bond created because of it is the throughline and content of the prophetic tradition in the Hebrew Bible and is the thematic link that makes it such a cohesive whole in the biblical corpus. While the ecstatic prophets appear now and then, it is the more soberminded criticizer and encourager who remains consistent throughout

---

2. Brueggemann, *The Prophetic Imagination*, 6.

3. Brueggemann, *The Prophetic Imagination*, 6–7. Emphasis in the original.

4. Previously in the chapter, Brueggemann refers to the criticizing function of the prophet as the "liberal tendency" and the energizing function as the "conservative tendency." See page 3 of *The Prophetic Imagination*. This dual prophetic function will appear in the call of Jeremiah as "to destroy" and "to rebuild" (Jer 1:10).

the Hebrew tradition and proves to be more effective in their prophetic endeavors. While both realities make their way into the New Testament, John the Baptist and Jesus of Nazareth are both much more in line with the "forthtelling" tradition rather than the "foretelling," even if the latter is not completely absent from their ministries.

John the Baptist criticizes the sin of Herod and bears witness to the alternative righteousness of God and confirms his belief through the witness of his life in martyrdom. Jesus criticizes the hypocrisy of the religious leaders of Judaism and offers a radically new way of envisioning the kingdom of God and confirms its truth in the witness of his life in martyrdom. The truth of his life and witness are vindicated by God through his resurrection. Peter and Paul, the leaders of the New Testament church after Jesus' resurrection, likewise, boldly shine light upon the waywardness of both Jews and Gentiles and articulate the new creation accomplished by God through the death and resurrection of Christ . . . and do so through the witness of their lives in martyrdom as well. Criticizing and energizing with bold conviction is the consistent work of the prophetic Spirit throughout Sacred Scripture.

DEFINING CHARACTERISTICS

With Brueggemann's help, the biblical prophets and their concerns come into clear focus. Here are a few of the most pertinent aspects of the prophetic spirituality gleaned from the texts of scripture:

- The prophet is one Spirit-inspired *to witness to the alternative reality revealed by the one God of righteousness* over against the prevailing, often dominant, unrighteous religious and political systems.
- The prophetic function is at once to both *criticize* and to *encourage*.
- As one who criticizes, the prophet seeks to *tear down* and *destroy* unrighteous religious and social systems. As one who encourages, the prophet seeks to *rebuild* righteous systems.
- It is possible for a prophet *to focus too much on criticizing* and not enough on encouraging or vice/versa. *Balance* is not guaranteed and must always be discerned.
- *Risk* and *courage* and two dominant characteristics of prophets.
- Prophets often bear witness to their vision through *martyrdom*.

- As *seers* and *visionaries*, prophets have lively *imaginations* of what can be, and, through divine inspiration, speak forth and embody *new realities* and, thus, offer *hope*.
- The vision of the new reality, the kingdom of God, has a specific content . . . it is a way of being that reflects the life of God where *justice*, *peace*, and *charity* prevail.
- *Discernment* and *decisiveness* are two important functions within the prophetic dimension and serve to allow the prophetic voice and/or action to be clearly communicated and firmly established.
- Not only is the pagan world the object of prophetic activity but also is the *people of God* by which they are called to constant *reformation* and *renewal*.
- As such, the prophetic dimension offers the church an integral source of *vitality* and *dynamism* and *guards her from stagnation and hypocrisy*.
- Being *maintained in truth* is the work of the prophetic Spirit.

THE PROPHETIC DIMENSION IN CHURCH HISTORY

The Age of the Martyrs

As the Greek *martyrein* conveys the meaning of "bearing witness," it would make sense that the early Christians would understand the act of martyrdom as fundamentally an evangelical, sacramental, and prophetic act. It was a way of proclaiming the gospel, participating in the gospel, and of revealing the gospel in one heroic act of embodied belief. The ancient Christians who suffered for the sake of Christ, though not to the point of death, were called "confessors." What confessors and martyrs demonstrated by their acts of suffering and death was their firmness of belief and conviction of faith. These acts would confer courage and inspiration for others who would come to face similar dilemmas during periods of persecution.

As we have seen in our glimpse at the Hebrew prophets, one of the common results of the prophet's call for reform and fidelity was persecution and martyrdom. Instead of the word of the prophet being silenced by such persecution and martyrdom, it was often the case that the opposite effect would in fact occur. Instead of silence, the act of undergoing persecution, suffering, and death for the sake of Christ had a way of amplifying the prophet's word and cause. In this sense, the act of martyrdom is in itself a prophetic act of revealing the content of the prophet's faith that bears an enduring power and force.

In continuity with the prophetic acts of denunciation and annunciation, of tearing down and building up, martyrs, with the undeniable proclamation of their lives, denounce and tear down the systems of injustice that seek to militate against the establishment of the kingdom of God and announce and build up the very kingdom of God for which they lived and died. Their blood, as seed, is life-giving. Their death is birth. What the martyr professed is made flesh and immortalized in the seal of the martyr's blood and attains a transcendent power which speaks with greater conviction than words alone can communicate.

Above all, Christian martyrdom witnesses to the truth of the primacy of love above all other realities. Dying for Christ is dying for all that Christ proclaimed, including his vision of the kingdom of God. In extension, dying for Christ is a participation in his prophetic role of revealing this kingdom through his death. In what is widely considered the most important treatise on martyrdom that the church has produced, Origen, in his *Exhortation to Martyrdom*, reflects that martyrs are motivated most of all by so great a love that they are willing to even pay the price of separation that this love at times demands, even to the point of the severing of one's soul from one's body. They are moved by a vigorous sense of honor and duty to repay God with what God deserves in giving so much to humankind. It is the fulfillment of the Christian's baptismal covenant and its highest expression. And, most strikingly, for Origen, the blood of the martyrs contains the power to ransom, just as Christ's blood. Martyrdom, therefore, for Origen, besides being evangelical, sacramental, and prophetic, is also mystical.

Prophetic Enthusiasm, Early Ascetic Movements, and Monastic Reform

Early Christianity boasted both dimensions of the prophetic robustly within its life, the charismatic "foretelling" and the type of prophetic "forthtelling" highlighted in this chapter. Montanism, one of the most visible and controversial movements to arise in the late second century, became known as the "New Prophecy" by its adherents. Because of their belief and practice of active prophetic revelations coupled with wild ecstatic behavior, they became labeled as heretics by the wider church. Pentecostal prophecy was not uncommon or controversial in of itself in the second century church. What ostracized the "New Prophecy" was its claim that the prophet was directly inspired by the Holy Spirit, fully possessed by God, blurring the distinction between human and divine in the life of the prophet, along with the highly spontaneous, erratic frenzy of the prophetic moment. Eusebius would later describe Montanus himself disparagingly, "And he [Montanus] became beside himself, and being suddenly in a sort of frenzy and ecstasy, he raved, and began to babble and utter strange things, prophesying in a manner contrary to the constant custom of the Church handed down by tradition from the beginning."[5]

The controversy surrounding pentecostal prophecy at this moment in the church's history would help lead to its eventual suppression, only popping up here and there throughout the subsequent centuries until, of course, the beginning of the twentieth century with the revitalization of the pentecostal movement throughout the church. But the negative suspicion directed toward pentecostal prophecy would contribute, in effect, to the suppression of the other prophetic roles of the church as well, due to the blurring of the lines between pentecostal prophecy and the broader prophetic dimension of the church. Yet, there was another mitigating factor that marginalized the prophetic dimension: the alignment with the church with the empire.

The prophetic dimension, whose soil is always found most fertile on the periphery of society, and, often, on the periphery of the institutional church, was largely made obsolete after the Edict of Milan when, in 313, Christianity ceased to be a persecuted minority but an accepted component of the Roman Empire. The prophetic witness of the age of the martyrs nearly vanished overnight, and the world, the object of prophetic witness, was rapidly becoming sacralized. Or was it?

This paradigm shift in the life of the church, indeed the Western world, would radically change the function of the prophetic. If before 313 the prophetic witness of the church was aimed predominantly at the pagan world, after 313, the prophetic witness of the church would be aimed at not only the pagan world outside the church but also at a worldly church. Movements within the church would begin distancing themselves from the wider church, with the intention of preserving the original fervor, commitment, and witness of the persecuted Christians during the age of the martyrs. This voluntary marginalization manifested itself in various ascetic

5. Eusebius of Caesarea, "Church History, Book V."

movements which would quickly organize itself into the monastic movement which rapidly spread throughout the empire during the fourth and fifth centuries. Monasticism, as the church on the margins witnessing to the values of the kingdom of God in its common life and in its solitude with God, served as the major preserver of the prophetic dimension of the church for these centuries, until, of course, monasticism itself began to retreat from the margins and cozy itself up with the wider church and world. The monastic reform movements of the tenth and eleventh centuries did much to recover the prophetic posture of the church, yet, it was only a matter of time when these movements would also need reform.

Ecclesia semper reformanda est ("the church must always be reformed"), a saying attributed to St. Augustine, aptly captures the prophetic spirit alive in the church. This prophetic spirit seeks to continually recapture the original radical fidelity to God demanded of the gospel that the prophetic tradition has always sought. The church, made up of sinful human beings, has proven that it consistently slips away from its covenantal commitments and, thus, equally constantly needs the witness of the prophets to call it back to fidelity. Thomas Merton would, in fact, define the prophet as simply one who is faithful to God. Fidelity to God means fidelity to the values of God's kingdom revealed to us in Christ and his gospel. Implicit in fidelity to such a commitment is the critique of all that does not align with these values. The prophetic dimension of the church, in this light, is the dimension of the church that calls for action, for pronouncements, and for decision. It compares the realities of the church and the world with the ultimate values of the kingdom and demands conformity at whatever cost. It functions as the conscience of the church and world constantly holding out a vision of what each can be. It possesses an intrinsic eschatological thrust and sees complacency as one of the greatest threats to ecclesial vitality. This evolved understanding of the prophetic role of the church would help the church in her commitment to the values of the kingdom and would help her see more clearly her prophetic priorities in her relationship to the world. These prophetic priorities would coalesce in potent ecclesial movements in the twentieth century and would set the church off into new directions it had not yet explored with great interest or concern up until this point.

THE CONSCIENCE OF THE CHURCH

The Social Gospel and Catholic Social Teaching

The Social Gospel was a prominent movement that arose within Protestantism in the United States and Canada in the early twentieth century. It sought to address the social injustices of the time, which included issues of poverty, economic inequality, racism, education, war, and crime, among others. The teachings of Jesus in the Gospels, particularly the Lord's Prayer which prayed for the kingdom of God to come on earth as it is in heaven, were the theological heartbeat of the movement. Its proponents were mostly a part of the liberal wing of the church, including Richard T. Ely, Josiah Strong, Washington Gladden, and Walter Rauschenbusch, though the movement can be traced back to Henry George's work *Progress and Poverty*, which sparked the single tax movement.[6]

One of the movement's most notable proponents, Walter Rauschenbusch, would write prolifically about the ideals of the movement and do much to promote those ideals. In his 1917 work, *A Theology of the Social Gospel*, Rauschenbusch argued that Christians, especially Protestants, had too often interpreted the gospel individualistically and focused too myopically on individual sinfulness. He sought to shed light on social, institutionalized sinfulness which lead to the oppression and extortion of groups within society. The notion of the "Kingdom of God" formed the theological heartbeat of Rauschenbusch's book. Distinguishing between the "Kingdom of God" and the church, Rauschenbusch argued that the "Kingdom of God" was not subject to the weaknesses of the church but tests and corrects the church and serves as the prophetic, social, and political force within the church. Rauschenbusch also advocated that Christians should imitate God who, in Christ, came to serve all equally without discrimination. Martin Luther King, Jr. would cite the Social Gospel as one of the main sources of inspiration for his own prophetic ministry in his fight for social justice.

During the same period that North American Protestantism was developing its social conscience in the Social Gospel movement, the conscience of the Roman Catholic Church, too, was being formed. The publication of Pope Leo XIII's encyclical *Rerum novarum* in 1891 began the accumulation of an impressive body of work that continues to this day with the publication of Pope Francis' notable encyclical *Laudato si'* of 2015. Some of the primary principles of Catholic social teaching gleaned from

---

6. The single tax movement was an economic ideology which held that the economic rent coming from land should belong to all members of society equally.

this body of work are human dignity (based on being created in the image and likeness of God), subsidiarity (never assigning to a greater or higher association what lesser or subordinate organizations can do), solidarity and the common good (each person is interdependent upon the whole of humanity and creation), charity (the foundation for every responsibility and commitment), and social justice (addressing social and economic injustices that lead to the oppression of individuals and communities).

Pope Francis has notably focused much of his pontificate advocating for both social and ecclesial change. In his Apostolic Exhortation, *Evangelii gaudium*, which sent seismic shockwaves through the Roman Catholic Church with rippling effects throughout the world, Francis is in full prophetic mode. The second paragraph of the encyclical reads:

> The great danger in today's world, pervaded as it is by consumerism, is the desolation and anguish born of a complacent yet covetous heart, the feverish pursuit of frivolous pleasures, and a blunted conscience. Whenever our interior life becomes caught up in its own interests and concerns, there is no longer room for others, no place for the poor. God's voice is no longer heard, the quiet joy of his love is no longer felt, and the desire to do good fades. This is a very real danger for believers too. Many fall prey to it, and end up resentful, angry and listless. That is no way to live a dignified and fulfilled life; it is not God's will for us, nor is it the life in the Spirit which has its source in the heart of the risen Christ.[7]

While Francis focuses his attention on attacking the sin of consumerism and unjust economic systems in *Evangelii gaudium*, sin against the environment is the object of his attack in *Laudato si'*:

> "LAUDATO SI', mi' Signore" – "Praise be to you, my Lord". In the words of this beautiful canticle, Saint Francis of Assisi reminds us that our common home is like a sister with whom we share our life and a beautiful mother who opens her arms to embrace us. "Praise be to you, my Lord, through our Sister, Mother Earth, who sustains and governs us, and who produces various fruit with coloured flowers and herbs".
>
> This sister now cries out to us because of the harm we have inflicted on her by our irresponsible use and abuse of the goods with which God has endowed her. We have come to see ourselves as her lords and masters, entitled to plunder her at will. The violence present in our hearts, wounded by sin, is also reflected in the

---

7. Pope Francis, *Evangelii gaudium*.

> symptoms of sickness evident in the soil, in the water, in the air and in all forms of life. This is why the earth herself, burdened and laid waste, is among the most abandoned and maltreated of our poor; she "groans in travail" (*Rom* 8:22). We have forgotten that we ourselves are dust of the earth (cf. *Gen* 2:7); our very bodies are made up of her elements, we breathe her air and we receive life and refreshment from her waters.[8]

These prophetic concerns of Pope Francis are corroborated by his general interest in the nature of the prophetic within the life of the church. In a homily given in the Vatican's Casa Santa Marta on December 16, 2013, the pontiff pointed specifically to the task of the true prophet:

> . . . a prophet is someone who listens to the words of God, who reads the spirit of the times, and who knows how to move forward towards the future. True prophets hold within themselves three different moments: past, present, and future. They keep the promise of God alive, they see the suffering of their people, and they bring us the strength to look ahead. God looks after his people by giving them prophets in the hardest times, in the midst of their worst suffering.[9]

Martin Luther King, Jr., Oscar Romero, and Liberation Theology

Perhaps the most notable prophetic witness that the church has raised up in the modern era has been the civil rights pastor Martin Luther King, Jr. (1929–1968). It is widely acknowledged across denominational lines that Martin Luther King, Jr. exercised a prophetic ministry resembling the prophets of Ancient Israel.[10] In a January 16, 2009 address celebrating Martin Luther King, Jr, Carlyle Fielding Stewart, III highlighted ten points of correspondence between the Hebrew prophets and King. He argues:

---

8. Francis, *Laudato si'*.

9. Quoted in Arcement, *In the School of Prophets: The Formation of Thomas Merton's Prophetic Spirituality*, 207.

10. Joseph Milburn Thompson, in his 1981 doctoral dissertation, "Martin Luther King, Jr. and Christian Witness: An Interpretation of King Based on a Theological Model of Prophetic Witness," at Fordham University, argued (unconvincingly, in my opinion) against interpreting Martin Luther King, Jr. as a "prophet" in line with the prophets of Ancient Israel.

1. King's ministry was prophetic because his leadership was transformational, rooted in the vision of the kingdom of God . . . in the idea of a God of love and justice who is concerned for the poor and oppressed.

2. King's ministry was prophetic because he stood in the Mosaic tradition of Exodus liberation.

3. King's type of rhetoric was reminiscent of biblical prophetic speech.

4. King boldly spoke truth to power challenging the power establishments in both church and government.

5. King, unlike the court prophets or shamanistic prophets of old, was a free prophet who stood on the institutional periphery in order to provoke change.

6. King was moved by the pathos of God. He deeply felt the overwhelming sympathy and compassion of God for oppressed humankind and was moved to act as intercessor on their behalf.

7. King, as a free prophet, called all people to enjoy the covenantal relationship which is the right of all made in God's image and likeness and envisioned a beloved community where justice, freedom, truth, and equality were afforded to all.

8. King challenged both governments and churches to transform themselves into agents of social change thus placing their power and influence at the service of the most vulnerable of society.

9. King accepted the dangers that came with his prophetic responsibilities and did not shy away from them.

10. King, as prophet, stood in the best of the old covenant traditions, always calling the people back to God and to their responsibility to make the world a more just and equitable place.[11]

King, of course, would also tragically follow after many in the prophetic tradition who validate their witness through the gift of their life for their cause when on April 4, 1968 he would be gunned down while standing on his hotel balcony in Memphis, Tennessee. The movement he inspired continues its leavening work throughout today's churches and societies offering greater freedom and justice to multitudes, even while continuing

---

11. Stewart, III, "Martin Luther King, Jr. as Modern Prophet: Some Similarities with the Ancient Prophets of Israel."

to incite animosity from those threatened by his vision of radical inclusivity and equality.

The former Roman Catholic Archbishop of San Salvador, Oscar Romero (1917–1980), was assassinated on March 24, 1980 at the age of 62; shot, while celebrating Mass, for his radical solidarity with the poor and his outspoken defense on their behalf. The death of his priest-friend, Rutilio Grande, SJ, was a pivotal moment for Romero to move out into the prophetic arena and to more courageously speak out against the state violence being perpetrated against the poor. Intuiting his impending death, Romero would make this prophetic statement: "If they kill me, I will rise again in the Salvadoran people."[12] Of this paschal prophecy, Margaret Swedish would write, "Romero, then, has risen in his people because he reflected back to them their own story, their faith, their reality. At the same time, the people rose and continue to rise in Romero, for it was their inspiration, their courage, their martyrdom, their faith and witness, that inspired him to become a pastor at their service."[13] The Jesuit theologian, Jon Sobrino, calls attention to the sacramental dimension of Romero's prophetic witness: "I believe that for them, for me and for many others, Monseñor Romero was an actualized Christ and, as Christ, a sacrament of God. To confront oneself with Romero was like confronting oneself with God. To encounter Monseñor Romero in one's personal life was as encountering God. To try to follow Monseñor Romero was to follow Jesus today in El Salvador."[14] As the ancient prophets were the "conscience of Israel," Romero became the "conscience of El Salvador." In the words of the late Pope Benedict XVI, writing in the 1970s, the prophets were able "to probe deeper than the slogans of the day, who see more than others because they embrace a wider reality;"[15] an apt description of Romero's sacrificial commitment to the kingdom of God.

Oscar Romero's inspiring solidarity with the poor and oppressed shares similar concerns with the theological and social movement in the church at this time, particularly that of Latin American Catholicism. Although Romero was quite critical of liberation theology during the early years of his ministry, he exhibited a growing appreciation of its ideals and concerns, especially after the death of Rutilio Grande. Romero's early concern was the

12. Cited in Swedish, "Oscar Arnulfo Romero: Prophet to the Americas."
13. Swedish, "Oscar Arnulfo Romero: Prophet to the Americas."
14. Cited in Swedish, "Oscar Arnulfo Romero: Prophet to the Americas."
15. Cited in Battle, "Romero: A Prophet for Our Time."

concern that many in the church have had about this movement: that it is steeped in Marxism and that it justifies and encourages violence. Others argue that such a reading of liberation theology is only a caricature. As a movement, to the extent that it is not integrally understood and realized, the danger has been to drift toward these caricatures. But integrally understood and realized, liberation theology has been a major force to awaken the prophetic dimension of the church.

In his article, "Archbishop Oscar Romero and Liberation Theology," the German Jesuit Martin Maier identifies three basic principles of liberation theology:

1. The church's option for the poor
2. The church's attention to the signs of the times
3. The church's contribution to change the world, not just to understand it[16]

The church's commitment to the poor, for Maier, is grounded in the belief that every human being is made in the image and likeness of God. God demonstrated this commitment to the poor in the acts of incarnation and *kenosis* (self-emptying on the cross), the full solidarity of the divine with broken humanity. In the church's attention to the signs of the times, it seeks to be vigilant about seeking the will of God amidst the changing circumstances of history. It cuts through the cacophony of ideologies that social media barrages the public with and boldly speaks the truth into the chaos, thus stabilizing it. The church's contribution to change the world, not just understand it, makes its commitments authentic and demonstrates its prophetic power.

Matthew Ashley, in his article, "Liberation Spirituality," in *The New Westminster Dictionary of Christian Spirituality*, begins by stating that "Liberation theology can refer to a large family of theologies... that focus on the superation of unjust social, political and economic structures as an *integral* part of Christian faith."[17] Ashley goes on to note three aspects that liberation spirituality stresses: (1) the need to resist and overcome the restriction of spirituality to a small group of Christian elites; (2) the need to resist and overcome spirituality's privatization; (3) the need to resist and overcome

---

16. Maier, "Archbishop Oscar Romero and Liberation Theology."

17. Ashley, "Liberation Spirituality," in *The New Westminster Dictionary of Christian Spirituality*, 406. Emphasis added.

spirituality's excessive interiorization.[18] In light of these astute observations, it is easy to see the gift liberation theology has been to spirituality and vice versa. Today, the liberation theology movement has expanded far beyond its Latin American provenance and seeks to bear prophetic witness on behalf of other oppressed groups based on race, gender, and sexual orientation. Ecological issues have become, more recently, a major concern as well.

Ashley also notes the growing development of liberation spirituality's connection with martyrdom. He notes that this is not surprising "given the fate of countless thousands of Chrsitans who lived this spirituality and were murdered for it by the state."[19] It makes sense, then, he points out, that Oscar Romero would become a type of patron saint from which many of the oppressed would draw hope.

TOWARD AN INTEGRAL PROPHETIC ECCLESIAL SHAPE

Both conservatives and progressives claim the prophetic dimension of the church as their own. In my mind, both are justified in doing so. Conservatives understand the prophetic dimension largely in terms of fidelity to the Word of God in a world that has mostly forgotten it. This approach has solid precedence in the prophetic literature of the Hebrew Bible. They see the future in terms of an ideal past without which the church will lose its anchor and stability and will become susceptible to drifting outside the straight and narrow path that leads to God. Progressives understand the prophetic dimension largely in terms of social justice. This approach is also based on solid biblical grounds as is seen in the prophetic literature. They see the future in terms of an ideal present where the church's number one priority should be the righting of all wrongs and the liberating of all oppressed. Part of understanding the integral nature of the prophetic dimension of the church is to insist upon keeping these two approaches united. The conservative approach grounds the church's social justice agendas in the Christian theological, spiritual tradition and helps direct and empower it. The progressive approach protects the insistence on fidelity to the Word

---

18. Ashley, "Liberation Spirituality," in *The New Westminster Dictionary of Christian Spirituality*, 406.

19. Ashley, "Liberation Spirituality," in *The New Westminster Dictionary of Christian Spirituality*, 407.

of God from slipping into an ideology without regard to the circumstances and struggles of real human beings.

In relation to the other dimensions of the church, the prophetic dimension, as the conscience of the church, keeps the church firmly in tune with reality. It discerns the movements of society in light of revelation and justice and boldly and courageously, and sometimes sacrificially, seeks to bring society in line with these two poles of truth. In doing so, the prophetic dimension of the church serves to realize the kingdom of God in the world as much as possible. It also serves as a corrective to the church itself, particularly the institutional apparatus of the church, to make sure that it is in no way placing a stumbling block in the way of this realization and is always oriented toward the further realization of God's kingdom. In regard to the six other dimensions of the church, the prophetic dimension helps the evangelical dimension reincarnate itself and speak to current issues with relevancy and illumination; it helps the pentecostal dimension expand its understanding and experience of the prophetic beyond spiritual phenomena and ecstatic utterance; it helps the sacramental dimension see its symbolic and communal potential for revealing injustice and realizing the "beloved community;" it helps the intellectual dimension to think critically about the social problems of the day and helps give a language that effectively addresses them; it helps the mystical dimension use its clear vision to see through the illusions and fabrications of broken societies; it helps the pastoral dimension to always balance its ministry of mercy with the call to justice and fidelity to the Word of God.

The prophetic dimension well integrated into the life of the church will help the conservative wing pay better attention to the marginalized and oppressed and will help the progressive wing pay better attention to Christian revelation. The church today, particularly as it deals with the present culture wars and the social media which fuels them, suffers from the threat of polarization and further fragmentation. Both conservatives and progressives claim to be the true prophets of the kingdom of God. An integral understanding of the church, as I see it, is the way to redirect this growing bifurcation to a place that is healthy and whole. A truly prophetic church is neither conservative nor progressive, it is integral (both conservative and progressive maturely integrated).

CHAPTER 8

An Integral Church

A CHURCH WHOSE TIME HAS COME

The call for an integral church is not a call for another movement within the church but a call for the integration of all movements of the church into one, to the extent that these movements add to the church's overall catholicity. Such an integration would give birth to a more mature ecclesial shape which would evidence a greater ecclesial unity and, thus, serve both the gospel and the world with greater effectiveness. It is a call to another paradigm shift within the life of the church where the dialectical relationship of the seven dimensions gives birth to a new integral consciousness of ecclesial wholeness and catholicity. This birthing is happening, and this book was written to help further serve this cause.

How did we arrive at such a time as this? This awakening to a higher, more integral ecclesial consciousness did not simply drop out of heaven into our particular moment in history. What we are now experiencing here in the early years of the twenty-first century is the result of a long process of development, often through very painful birth pangs. I hope that some of this process is made clearer through the various movements which have been sketched in this book. The most significant movement in recent years that deserves special mention, though, is the ecumenical movement that characterized much of the twentieth century and opened the various Christian denominations and ecclesial movements to a more friendly and benevolent stance toward one another. The dialogue which the movement called for has served as a catalyst to building greater appreciation among the various churches and the alleviation of much suspicion and animosity.

Full communion is now being realized between churches who have historically been separate. Roman Catholics and Protestants, far from condemning each other *de facto,* as in time past, are finding elements in each other to admire and emulate. The east is now in the west and the west in the east and each is, thankfully, finding it more difficult to remain isolated in their own ecclesial cocoons. Of course, ecumenism isn't the only catalyst to explain this current phenomenon of integration, *globalization* is perhaps the underlying cause and indispensable prerequisite for this evolutionary moment, including ecumenism itself.[1]

THREATS TO AN INTEGRAL CHURCH

Globalization, as is seen in society as well as church, brings with it not only potential for fostering greater unity but also for fostering greater dissension and strife. The coming together of groups always poses a threat to identity preservation and the psychological need for stability. The power of unquestioned ideology fueled by media systems which validate one worldview while vilifying another has served to protect groups from the supposed threat of the other, keeping them trapped in their own limited identities and illusory stabilities. The expansion of an either/or, dualistic consciousness which defaults to an "us *vs* them" competitiveness toward a more mature both/and, unitive consciousness which defaults to an "us *and* them" communion of cooperation and appreciation is the only way forward toward the realization of the beloved community of the kingdom of God. An integral church is not a church of uniform belief and worship. It is a church of unity in diversity, with diversity being a constitutive part of the church's unity and a sign of its strength, not an unfortunate concession afforded to a sinful branch of the church.

On the conservative side of the ideological spectrum, fundamentalism and traditionalism pose the greatest threats to the realization of an integral church and keep believers trapped in their either/or, dualistic ways of thinking and being. On the progressive side, a liberal dismissiveness which ignores the voices of scripture and tradition and throws out all criterion for ecclesial belonging also shirks the responsibility of integral wholeness. It is this unchecked liberalism which, in fact, helped give rise to radical forms

---

1. See Rausch's *Towards a Truly Catholic Church* (Collegeville, MN: Liturgical Press, 2005), especially Chapter 9, "A Truly Catholic Church," for an insightful understanding of the effects of globalization on the contemporary church.

of fundamentalism. An integral church needs conservative and progressive voices to exist in a healthy dialectical relationship. What it cannot and should not tolerate are extremist voices which are fueled by ideological presuppositions which give no space in themselves for the other.

THE NEED FOR AN INTEGRAL CHURCH

While it cannot be assumed that all Christians and ecclesial communities desire greater unity and are willing to invest in the ecumenical dialogue which serves as its prerequisite, it is safe to assume that all Christians and ecclesial communities desire a healthy church, even if the more radical free church tradition denies the existence of a universal, "catholic" dimension to the church and sees the church purely in localized, particular communities. It is hard to imagine a Christian in an independent evangelical church not hoping for a healthier Roman Catholic Church and vice versa. This desire for health and wholeness can, perhaps, serve as the starting point for constructing a way toward a truly integral church. This assumes that an integral church, as this book has presupposed and has tried to demonstrate, is a healthier church than one fragmented into ecclesial denominations that ignore or vilify one another. A vision of a church whose members truly love one another and seek to know one another better ought to be a vision for every ecclesial body. It is part of the gospel demand and what it means to be a Christian participating in the life of the Trinity. The ultimate realization of wholeness is up to God; the desire and demand for this realization is largely up to us (in cooperation with God's Spirit who always seeks to draw together in love).

The church in the twenty-first century struggles with an integrity issue. Many of its leaders have exhibited scandalous behavior that has discredited the church's witness and many non-Christians now look upon the church as fueling hate and bigotry by its judgmentalism and lack of pastoral sense. While these accusations may serve as an excuse to some, to ignore them altogether would only serve to drag the church further down into the mire of irrelevance and disrepute. What the world needs is a church that is mature and knows how to converse with the world in such ways that exhibit its integrity and maturity. The only way to restore credibility in the church is through integral wholeness. A juvenile church that throws tantrums when it doesn't get its way with the world will never do anything to change it. An integral church is a church which knows how to listen to all voices and discriminates against none. It finds the truth in each claim it hears and kindly discards what is deemed untrue. It can prophetically denounce what is wrong because it has previously announced what is right and good with care and compassion. It is trusted because it is known to be sensitively caring and authentically concerned. It is heard because it is known that its personal interests always come last. There is only one way for the church to arrive at such maturity and self-possession: if it cultivates its full dimensionality which would, thus, afford it the grace to be such in the world.

THE INSTITUTIONAL CHURCH

As mentioned in the Introduction, this study has intentionally focused on the spirituality of the church. In so doing, the institutional component of the church, although closely related, has been outside the purview of our concern. Yet, the question arises as to what relationship do the seven dimensions of ecclesial spirituality have with the institutional structure of the church. It is frequently quipped that the institutional church should be at the service of the charismatic church. This quip seeks to convey that the governing branch of the church should facilitate the work of the Spirit and be careful not to impede it. This is spoken from hindsight, in a sense, having lived through epochs of the church's history when an exaggerated institutional church is perceived to have done just this—to have stifled the work of the Spirit through unnecessary bureaucracy and self-interest in protecting the power and prestige of the institution. This concern is no longer heard only from the radical reformers of the free church tradition but from Roman Catholics steeped in a highly institutional tradition. While the quip may be a bit too curt and simplistic, it does convey a truth to which it would be wise to adhere. The seven dimensions of ecclesial spirituality is the dynamism of the church which the institutional component of the church should seek to govern and nurture. The church as an institution, which I see as a necessary component of the church rooted mainly in the sacramental and pastoral dimensions and issuing from them, becomes dysfunctional precisely when it begins to function as a separate entity from the seven dimensions. It is not our concern here to opine which shape the church as an institution should take. What is crucially necessary is that the governing body of the church be always integrally related to the spiritual dynamism of its seven dimensions.

In this way, the governing apparatus of the church will be oriented toward its mission as facilitating the kingdom of God here on earth. Its concern will be with the proclamation of the gospel, with demonstrating its reality in the power of the Spirit, with awakening those so called to an embodied, sacramental way of being, with passing on the wisdom of the tradition, with participating in the divine life, with pastoral care and concern, and with working for justice and peace. This is the job description of the governing church, which it should be very careful not to obfuscate. The power that it is granted should always be at the service of this mission. The danger, which we have learned from experience, is that the work of reconciliation to which the governing church is commissioned is often sidelined for other reasons, be they reasons motivated by self-preservation, by egocentric clericalism, or by the fear of scandal. As the body of Christ in the world, of which the governing body of the church is called to be an integral member, the church must govern in the Spirit of its Christ—with humility, conviction, wisdom, and self-sacrifice.

THE CURRENT SHAPE OF THE CHURCH

What do the current trends shaping the church today tell us about the church's integrity and wholeness at this present moment in the church's history? In the West, secularization has drastically impacted the numbers of active, church-going Christians. This is particularly true in mainline Protestant denominations. Roman Catholicism in the US is buttressed by Roman Catholic immigrants, mainly from Latin America. Churches in Canada and Europe are largely empty on Sundays. Where the church is experiencing current growth is mainly through the influence of pentecostalism and the charismatic movement it has spurred. This is especially true of the church in the southern hemisphere, notably South America and Africa.

Yet, it must be emphasized that larger churches are not necessarily healthier, more integrated ones. Popularity does not make for maturity. It may well be that a smaller congregation demonstrates greater catholicity and wholeness than a "thriving" megachurch. Nevertheless, smaller churches should seek to understand what is so attractive about the churches which experience growth in today's secularized society. Surveys suggest that there are three primary causes for churches that grow: the sense of God's presence in worship, the sense of community, and good preaching. The sense of God's presence in worship is now appealing to both traditionalists who find high liturgical worship an effective way of evoking the transcendent and to charismatics who find praise and worship evoking the sense of God's nearness in an emotionally impactful way. Liturgical churches with uninspiring liturgies struggle with membership. Non-liturgical churches with uninspiring worship services will not likely last.

The integration of the ecclesial dimensions which is currently happening at this time in the church's history is seeing a greater emphasis on preaching and more careful planning of liturgies in Roman Catholic churches, just as a greater interest in liturgy and sacraments is currently happening in some historically non-liturgical churches. Roman Catholics, especially since Vatican II, are much more open to learning from evangelicals about what makes for effective ministry. This is particularly true in Roman Catholic youth ministry, which has blossomed in the past few generations and, in many cases, serves as a vitalizing force in Roman Catholic parishes. Also inspired by evangelicals, more Roman Catholic parishes are recognizing the need for developing a sense of community among parishioners and are employing methods which are suitable to their particular situation which supplement the liturgical experience.

If we assess each ecclesial dimension individually in the church today, we can say that the evangelical dimension, always a strong dimension in Protestantism, is particularly alive in evangelical and charismatic churches and is becoming a stronger dimension in Roman Catholic churches since Vatican II. The Orthodox Church in the east has experienced less influence from the Protestant emphasis of the content of the gospel. Yet, the Orthodox Church in the west is currently having a significant imputation of the evangelical dimension from evangelical converts to Orthodoxy. While this may be of benefit to helping make Orthodoxy a more integral community of churches, it must be noted that not every evangelical is a healthy, well-integrated evangelical. There may be resistance to the type of evangelicalism of these converts which may prevent mutual growth and enrichment for both the new convert and the existing communities who receive them. This is true of any convert, whether evangelical or any other emphasizing a particular dimension. Nevertheless, the blending of traditions which happens when individuals or groups convert from one tradition to another, while it may be for a time contentious or disruptive, has the potential, in the long run, of producing a more well-rounded ecclesial shape. Liberal Protestantism should take note that neglecting the content of the gospel and the foundational source of revelation that is the Bible because of elements in them which are deemed harmful or unjust could lead to a version of Christianity that more resembles a social activist group than a church. This is the major threat today among mainline Protestants who seek to recreate their identities based on an ideology of social justice that is not rooted in scripture and the Christian tradition.

The pentecostal dimension, as already mentioned, is the dimension, more than all the others, which is currently having its moment. After lying largely dormant for many centuries, the release of this dimension into the life of the church has been astonishing and quite revolutionary. It is certainly changing the shape of the church across the globe, leaving its impact on nearly every Christian tradition and creating a tradition of its own largely free from any oversight or governing restraints. For many Christians who have existed in more traditional communities, the encounter with the Spirit has been a source of revitalization and renewal—for them, personally, and for their communities. Others have decided that it would be better to leave their traditions and venture into the world of non-denominationalism and independence. From an integral perspective, legitimate concerns arise. The euphoric and emotional potency of the pentecostal dimension being experienced in the church today is particularly capable of luring many into its ambit at the expense of the other dimensions and thus threatening the balance of the church. Extremism is especially evident in independent churches with little to no oversight and has led to sincere believers forming ecclesial communities that indulge in spiritual experience and phenomena over the life of discipleship and service. Emotional manipulation and ego-driven charismatic leaders are the darker characteristics that the unhinged, unintegrated side of the contemporary pentecostal movement has produced. An integral perspective should, however, be careful not to dismiss this movement which has become such a source of blessing to so many in the church but should discern carefully the genuine aspects of it and seek to incorporate them in their own ecclesial life as seems best appropriate.

It would be difficult to overestimate the significance of the Second Vatican Council's contribution to the renewal of the sacramental dimension in the life of the church, both within Roman Catholicism and the other Christian traditions. *Sacrosanctum concilium* and the liturgical renewal movement of the twentieth century is currently paving a path toward significant progress in the work toward visible unity. A shared Eucharist is now a reality in many traditions and dialogue continues between the various Christian churches furthering mutual understanding and appreciation.

Non-liturgical churches are rediscovering the power of liturgy and ritual and the ecological crisis is opening up many Christians to the sacred preciousness of creation and its ability to reveal the divine. The fear of a faithless sacramentalism which was the concern of the reformers of the sixteenth century and led some to throw out the baby with the bathwater exerts a less potent bias against the sacramental life of the church, and their legitimate concerns are now being appreciated by liturgical Christians whose faith is being renewed through their encounter with the evangelical and pentecostal dimensions. Perhaps the time needed for some to throw off the perceived deadening effects of a faithless sacramentalism has run its course and these traditions are readying themselves to be renewed by the reintegration of the visible and concrete mediation of grace.

Also running its course is fundamentalism, the greatest threat to the intellectual dimension of the church. The shock of modernism that spurred the fundamentalist movement is subsiding and the Christians once lured into the simplistic thinking of literalism are beginning to appreciate thinking with nuance and depth. The integration of theology with science is revealing to be one of the most fecund sources of theological and spiritual reflection and the historical antagonism between them is becoming less pronounced. The insecurity which science and rational inquiry has afflicted upon many Christian communities is giving way to a new found stability that mature theological reflection wedded with these disciplines offers. The ecumenical movement has led to numerous denominational alliances which now pursue theological dialogue, several producing documents of agreement over topics which have separated Chrsitian traditions for centuries. Interdenominational theological consortiums now exist throughout the world which are serving to further build bridges between traditions and help Christians think with the whole mind of the church.

A widespread interest in spirituality is currently a main feature of Christian life. What matters most to many Christians is a way of life that is authentic and full of integrity. Hypocrisy and clericalism are no longer tolerated in many sectors of the church. The fear of the mystical, which has been a facet of the Protestant tradition, exerts far less power over younger generations who are being drawn into the experience of God found in silence and solitude. Monastic guest houses are now being populated by evangelicals and books on contemplative prayer are as popular among Protestants as they are among Roman Catholics and Orthodox. The need for groundedness and depth in an increasingly chaotic and superficial society is a universal need and is currently cutting through any bias of tradition or creed.

There are signs that the church is now maturing to the point when its pastoral dimension is being exercised without question or prerequisite. The unconditional love of God is now being felt the worldover. Even among evangelicals who have long regarded conversion as their main missionary objective, love for love's sake is now taking priority and is being understood as a vital and effective way of proclaiming the gospel. Ecumenical pastoral endeavors are now a regular feature of the contemporary church and demonstrate the fundamental ecclesial unity that already exists. The potential for greater shared pastoral ministry is one of the most tenable and attainable goals for deepening the ecumenical ties that now exist and for creating a more integral church.

As secularism further exerts its power over culture, the prophetic dimension of the church increasingly gains relevance and importance. As secular society increasingly exerts its power over the church and threatens its integrity, the prophetic dimension gains a crucial role in maintaining truth and ecclesial integrity. Fundamentalist isolationism has proven not to be the proper answer to secularism. Sometimes the world has something of great significance to teach the church, and God can as easily reveal truth to a non-Christian as to a Christian. Ecclesial discernment, then, is a necessary component and prerequisite to a mature prophetic church. This helps prevent the church from capitulating too quickly to society and the broad secular perspective of culture and philosophy, opting for a type of activism devoid of theological groundedness. The integrity of the church's prophetic dimension is contingent upon a healthy, yet, friendly distance from secularism, as well as from the elements within the church itself that have been infected by sin and injustice.

THE SHAPE OF THE CHURCH OF THE FUTURE

If all Christians can agree that the desire of God for the church is that it be healthy, mature, and as full of love as possible, then we can say that the desire of God for the church is that it be integral, alive in all its multi-dimensionality. What we are witnessing in this first half of the twenty-first century is the waning of denominationalism with its clear and distinct identities and the emergence of a greater catholicity with its inclusive embrace of the Christian tradition as a whole. Churches are more interested today in defining themselves by what they stand for than by what they stand against. Differentiation into denominationalism may have been a necessary part of the church's historical progress, but this differentiation, we are coming to see more clearly, was only the means to a further, deeper integration. The shape of the church of the future will then be characterized by this deeper integration and wholeness—a catholicity that is eager to embrace its multiple dimensions in order to live in the fullness of grace intended by God.

The church of the future will not be known as evangelical or pentecostal or sacramental. It will be a given that the three dimensions of initiation are equally integral to the whole. It will not be known for being overly intellectual or anti-intellectual. It will unhesitatingly embrace the mystical without the fear of losing its identity and groundedness. It will expand its pastoral ministry through collaboration without a litmus test to the Christian authenticity of one's fellow minister. It will work together as much as possible for the justice of God's kingdom to become a further reality here on earth and will challenge each other's communities, and one's own, to become more fully aligned with God's purposes and desires. It will discern together, and not only apart, the direction the Spirit leads in matters of faith, morals, and justice. It will, finally, learn that growth and mutual enrichment come when we place love above all else and trust one another's intention for God and the doing of God's will—when we finally relegate our judgmental prejudices to the dung heap of history where they belong. The fear of one Christian for another will have no place in the future shape of the church. The other will be seen as a gift and not a threat. Discernment and careful discrimination of the other will no longer lead to automatic animosity and suspicion but to dialogue and acceptance of differentiation.

The movements of the Spirit discerned in the biblical and historical tradition of the church in the pages of this book hopefully make it obvious that it is time for the Christian community to redirect its call away from the insistence that every ecclesial community looks the same (like our own particular ecclesial community!)—a form of ecclesial triumphalism where mine is always better than yours. In its place, we should begin the call for integration and wholeness and a new catholicity where differentiation and unity characterize a way of being together that more fully images the Divine Trinity—being constituted one precisely through differentiation in the single reality of love.

Bibliography

Arcement, Ephrem. *In the School of Prophets: The Formation of Thomas Merton's Prophetic Spirituality.* Collegeville, MN: Liturgical, 2015.
Ashley, Matthew. "Liberation Spirituality." In *The New Westminster Dictionary of Christian Spirituality*, ed. Philip Sheldrake. Louisville: Westminster John Knox, 2005.
Battle, John. "Romero: A Prophet for Our Time." https://www.leedsjp.org.uk/views/romero-a-prophet-for-our-time/.
Benedict XVI. *Deus caritas est.* https://www.vatican.va/content/benedict-xvi/en/encyclicals/documents/hf_ben-xvi_enc_20051225_deus-caritas-est.html.
Bertram, Robert. Review of *Christ the Sacrament of the Encounter with God*, by Edward Schillebeeckx. *Crossings*, https://crossings.org/review-of-edward-schillebeeckx-christ-the-sacrament-of-the-encounter-with-god/.
Brueggemann, Walter. *The Prophetic Imagination.* Minneapolis: Fortress, 2001.
———. *Theology of the Old Testament: Testimony, Dispute, Advocacy.* Minneapolis, MN: Fortress, 1997.
Cavarnos, Constantine and Mary-Barbara Zeldin. *Modern Orthodox Saints, 5: St. Seraphim of Sarov.* Belmont, MA: Institute for Byzantine and Modern Greek Studies, 1980.
Chesterton, G. K. *Saint Thomas Aquinas: The Dumb Ox.* NY: Image, 1956.
Chryssavgis, John. "Iconography." In *The New Westminster Dictionary of Christian Spirituality*, ed. Philip Sheldrake. Louisville: Westminster John Knox Press, 2005.
Congar, Yves. *The Holy Spirit in the 'Economy': Revelation and Experience of the Spirit*, vol. 1 of *I Believe in the Holy Spirit*. Translated by David Smith. New York: Crossroad, 2006.
Crenshaw, James L. *Education in Ancient Israel: Across the Deadening Silence.* NY: Doubleday, 1998.
Crouter, Richard. *Friedrich Schleiermacher: Between Enlightenment and Romanticism.* Cambridge: Cambridge University Press, 2005.
Daniélou, Jean. *From Glory to Glory: Texts from Gregory of Nyssa's Mystical Writings.* Crestwood, NY: St. Vladimir's Seminary Press, 2001.
Delio, Ilia. *Making All Things New: Catholicity, Cosmology, Consciousness.* Maryknoll: Orbis, 2015.
Drane, John. "Contemporary Culture and the Reinvention of Sacramental Spirituality." In *The Gestures of God: Explorations in Sacramentality*, ed. Geoffrey Rowell and Christine Hall. New York: Continuum, 2004.
Dreyer, Frederick A. *The Genesis of Methodism.* Bethlehem, N.J.: Lehigh University Press, 1999.

Eusebius of Caesarea. "Church History, Book V." New Advent. https://www.newadvent.org/fathers/250105.htm.

Fischer, Benjamin L. *Being a Pastor: Pastoral Treatises of John Wycliffe*. Translated by Benjamin L. Fischer. Landrum, SC: Davenant, 2021.

Francis, *Evangelii gaudium*. https://www.vatican.va/content/francesco/en/apost_exhortations/documents/papa-francesco_esortazione-ap_20131124_evangelii-gaudium.html#I.%E2%80%82A_joy_ever_new,_a_joy_which_is_shared.

———. *Laudato si'*. https://www.vatican.va/content/francesco/en/encyclicals/documents/papa-francesco_20150524_enciclica-laudato-si.html.

Gregory of Nazianzen. *Oration 39*. Translated by Charles Gordon Browne and James Edward Swallow. From *Nicene and Post-Nicene Fathers, Second Series*, Vol. 7. Edited by Philip Schaff and Henry Wace. Buffalo, NY: Christian Literature Publishing Co., 1894. Revised and edited for New Advent by Kevin Knight. <http://www.newadvent.org/fathers/310239.htm>.

Gregory the Great. *The Book of Pastoral Rule*. Translated by George E. Demacopoulos. Crestwood, NY: St. Vladimir's Seminary Press, 2007.

Hayward, C.J.S. "Symeon the New Theologian: On Faith." https://orthodoxchurchfathers.com/fathers/philokalia/symeon-the-new-theologian-on-faith.html.

Hofstedter, Richard. *Anti-Intellectualism in American Life*. NY: Vintage, 1963.

Ignatius of Antioch. "The Epistle to the Romans." In *Early Christian Writings*, translated by Maxwell Staniforth and Andrew Louth, 83–89. London: Penguin, 1987.

Irwin, Kevin W. "A Sacramental World–Sacramentality As The Primary Language for Sacraments. https://online.fliphtml5.com/ghag/ixpk.

Jeager, Werner. *Two Rediscovered Works of Ancient Christian Literature: Gregory of Nyssa and Macarius*. Leiden, Brill: 1954.

John Paul II. "Fides et ratio." http://www.vatican.va/content/john-paul-il/en/encyclicals/documents/hf_jp-ii_enc_14091998_fides-et-ratio.html.

Keating, Anna. "Why Evangelical Megachurches are Embracing (Some) Catholic Traditions." https://www.americamagazine.org/faith/2019/05/02/why-evangelical-megachurches-are-embracing-some-catholic-traditions.

Küng, Hans. *Great Christian Thinkers*. NY: Continuum, 2004.

Leinsle, Ulich G. *Introduction to Scholastic Theology*. Translated by Michael J. Miller. Washington, D.C.: The Catholic University of America Press, 2010.

McBrien, Richard. *Catholicism*. New York: HarperCollins, 1994.

Maier, Martin. "Archbishop Oscar Romero and Liberation Theology." http://www.romerotrust.org.uk/sites/default/files/MartinMaier1500words.pdf.

Merton, Thomas. *Conjectures of a Guilty Bystander*. NY: Doubleday, 1968.

Murk-Jansen, Saskia. *Brides in the Desert: The Spirituality of the Beguines*. Maryknoll, NY: Orbis, 1998.

"Nobel Committee: The Nobel Peace Prize 1979 press release." https://www.nobelprize.org/prizes/peace/1979/press-release/.

Noll, Mark. *The Scandal of the Evangelical Mind*. Grand Rapids, MI: Eerdmans, 1994.

Penduck, Joshua. "The Exciting Future of Evangelical Sacramentalism." https://openevangelical.wordpress.com/2017/06/07/the-exciting-future-of-evangelical-sacramentalism/.

Porete, Marguerite. *Marguerite Porete: The Mirror of Simple Souls*. Translated by Ellen L. Babinsky. New York: Paulist, 1993.

BIBLIOGRAPHY

Pseudo-Dionysius. *Pseudo-Dionysius: The Complete Works.* Translated by Colm Luibheid. NY, Paulist, 1987.

Rahner, Karl. *The Church and the Sacraments.* London: Nelson, 1963.

———. "Church and World." In *The Concise Sacramentum Mundi.* New York: Seabury, 1975.

Rausch, Thomas. *Towards a Truly Catholic Church.* Collegeville, MN: Liturgical, 2005.

Sacrosanctum Concilium, 59. https://docs.google.com/document/d/12Ai-BE4Iy3utFg0NROiWfqmDopiq2krp9j3VZmz4zpM/edit.

Schillebeeckx, Edward. *God the Future of Man.* New York: Sheed and Ward, 1968.

Schmemann, Alexander. *For the Life of the World.* Crestwood, NY: St. Vladimir's Seminary Press, 1963.

Seraphim of Sarov. "Saint Seraphim of Sarov: On the Acquisition of the Holy Spirit." http://www.orthochristian.com/47866.html.

Smith, Gordon T. *Evangelical, Sacramental, and Pentecostal: Why the Church Should Be All Three.* Downers Grove: IVP Academic, 2017.

Stewart, III, Carlyle Fielding. "Martin Luther King, Jr. as Modern Prophet: Some Similarities with the Ancient Prophets of Israel." https://www.carlylestewart.com/martin-luther-king-jr-as-modern-prophet-some-similarities-with-the-ancient-prophets-of-israel/.

Swedish, Margaret. "Oscar Arnulfo Romero: Prophet to the Americas." https://onlineministries.creighton.edu/CollaborativeMinistry/Martyrs/Romero/prophettoamericas.html.

Symeon the New Theologian. *Divine Eros: Hymns of Saint Symeon the New Theologian.* Translated by Daniel K. Griggs, Popular Patristics Series, Number 40. Crestwood: St. Vladimir's Seminary Press, 2010.

Teresa of Calcutta. "Mother Teresa: In Her Own Words." https://www.washingtonpost.com/wp-srv/inatl/longterm/teresa/stories/words.htm.

Tertullian. *Apology.* https://earlychurchtexts.com/public/tertullian_blood_christians_seed.htm.

Williams, A. N. *The Divine Sense: The Intellect in Patristic Theology.* Cambridge, UK: Cambridge University Press, 2007.

Index

Abalard, Peter, 81–82
Abbey of Gethsemani, 111–12
Abbey of Solesme, 59
Acts of the Apostles, 6
Adversus haereses (Irenaeus of Lyons), 77
Æthelberht, King, 13
Albertus Magnus, Saint, 82
Albigenses, 88
Aldersgate experience, 38
almsgiving, 120
Ambrose of Milan, Saint, 11, 119
American Catholicism, 90–91
American Revivalism, 37
Angela of Foligno, 108
Anglicanism, 58–59
Anglo-Catholicism, 59
anointings with oil, sacrament of, 51
Anselm of Canterbury, Saint, 81–82
Ante-Nicene Fathers, 77
Anthony of Egypt, Saint, 32–33
Anti-Intellectualism in American Life (Hofstadter), 89
anti-intellectualism of Fundamentalism, 88–92
apophaticism, 105
"Apostle to the Apostles," 3
"Apostle to the English," 13
"Apostle to the Gentiles," 3
"Apostle to the Germans," 3
"Apostles to the Slavs," 13
Apostolic Fathers, 77
"Archbishop Oscar Romero and Liberation Theology" (Maier), 144
Aristotle, 82

ascetic movements, early, 135–36
Ashley, Matthew, 144
Augustine, Benedictine monk, 13
Augustine of Hippo, Saint, 10–12, 80, 103, 119, 138
Authorized Version of the Bible, 58–59
Azusa Street Revival, 41

baptism
  after conversion, 9
  of infants/children, 56
  in the Spirit, 25, 41
  as a taking in, 53
Barth, Karl, 84–86
Basil of Caesars, Saint, 31–32
Beatrice of Nazareth, 108
Beauduin, Lambert, 60
Beguines (female lay movement), 108–9
Bell, Rob, 17
Benedict of Nursia, Saint, 35, 120
Benedict XVI, Pope, 18, 125, 126, 143
Bernard of Clairvaux, Saint, 81–82, 106–7, 109
bible
  Authorized Version of, 58–59
  Wycliffe translation of, 121
biblical inerrancy, 16
biblical theology, 75
bishops, central role of, 9
Black Death, 121
Bobbio Abbey, 13
Boersma, Hans, 67
Boethius, Saint, 81

INDEX

Bojaxhiu, Anjezë Gonxhe (later Mother Teresa), 124
Bonaventure, Saint, 35, 108
Boniface (Benedictine monk), 13
The Book of Common Prayer (1549), 58–59
Brueggemann, Walter, 50, 132–34, 133n4

Calvin, John, 56
Calvinism, 19
Campus Crusade for Christ,, 18
Cappadocians, 80, 103
Caroline Divines, 58–59, 67
Catholic Charismatic Renewal, 43–44
Catholic social teaching, 139–141
Catholicism. *See* Roman Catholic Church
Chantal, Jeanne de, 124
characteristics, defining
    evangelical dimension of the church, 6–9
    intellectual dimension, 74–77
    mystical dimension, 100–102
    pastoral dimension, 117–18
    Pentecostal dimension, 26–30
    prophetic dimension, 134–35
    scriptural dimension, 52–54
Charismatic Movement, 40–42, 41n10
charisms (spiritual gifts), 26, 43
charity, *Laudato si*,' 140
Chesterton, G. K., 82–83
Christ the Sacrament of the Encounter with God (Schillebeeckx), 63
Christian mysticism, 102
Christian nationalism, 16
Chryssavgis, John, 55–56
church history
    Anthony of Egypt, Saint, 32–33
    Augustine of Hippo, Saint, 10–12
    Barth, Karl, 84–86
    Basil of Caesars, Saint, 31–32
    Bernard of Clairvaux, Saint, 106–7
    Catholic Charismatic Renewal, 43–44
    Catholic social teaching, 139–141
    Charismatic Movement, 40–42
    Desert Fathers, 32–33

early ascetic movements, 135–36
English Reformation, 58–59
evangelical Catholicism, 17–18
evangelical dimension, 18–21
evangelical monks, 12–13
evangelical revival, 15–16
evangelicalism, contemporary trends, 16–17
Francis, Pope, 125–26
Francis de Sales, Saint, 123–24
fundamentalism, anti-intellectualism of, 88–92
Gregory of Nazianzus, Saint, 31–32
Gregory of Nyssa, Saint, 103–5
Gregory the Great, Saint (pope), 119–120
Hildegard of Bingen, Saint, 107–10
iconoclast controversy, 54–56
Ignatius of Antioch, Saint, 9–10
Ignatius of Loyola, Saint, 15
intellectual dimension, 77–92
Joachim of Fiore, 35–36
John Paul II, Saint (Pope), 86–88
John XXIII, Pope, 125–26
King, Martin Luther, Jr., 141–43
liberation theology, 143–45
Liturgical Movement, 59–61
Luther, Martin, 14
martyrs, age of, 135–36
Mendicant Movement, 14
Merton, Thomas, 111–13
monastic reform, 135–36
Montanism, 30–31
Mother Teresa of Calcutta, Saint, 124–25
mystical dimension, 103–13
Origen of Alexandria, 76–77
Orthodoxy, 18
Oxford movement, 58–59
pastoral dimension, 118–128
pastoral leadership, crisis in, 127–28
Patristic Period, 76–77
Pentecostalism, twentieth century, 40–42
Pietists, 36–37
prophetic dimension, 135–145
prophetic enthusiasm, 135–36
protestant fundamentalism, 16

INDEX

Pseudo-Dionysius, 105–6
Quakers, 36–37
Quietism, 110–11
Radical Reformation, 56–57
Rahner, Karl, 61–64
Romero, Oscar, Saint, 143, 145
sacramentality, 64–68
Schillebeeckx, Edward, 61–64
Schleiermacher, Friedrich, 84–86
Scholasticism, 80–84
Second Vatican Council,. *see* Second Vatican Council
Seraphim of Sarov, Saint, 38–40
social gospels, 139–141
Symeon the New Theologian Saint, 33–35
Thomas Aquinas, Saint, 80–84
Wesley, John, 37–38
Wyclif, John, 120–23
Cistercian reform, 57
Clement of Alexandria, Saint, 77
clericalism, 154
Columba, Saint (Irish monk), 12
Columbanus, Saint (Ireland), 13
Commentary on the Canticle of Canticles (Gregory of Nyssa), 103
common good, *Laudato si',* 140
communication of the gospel, 7
Confessio (Patrick, Saint), 13
Confessions (Augustine), 11–12, 103
Congar, Yves, 35–36, 37, 43–44
Constantine, Emperor, 18, 33, 118
Constitution on the Sacred Liturgy (Vatican II), 61–62
contemplative prayer, 154
Contra Celsum (Origen), 78
cosmic perspective, of created cosmos, 108
Council of Nicea (325), 77
Councils of the Church
    Council of Nicea (325), 77
    Seventh Ecumenical Council (787), 55
    Vatican Council I, 87
    Vatican Council II. *see* Second Vatican Council
Counter-Reformation Catholicism, 15, 120, 123

creation, cosmic perspective, 108
Crenshaw, James L., 72
Crouter, Richard, 85
Cyril, Saint, 13

Daniélou, Jean, 104–5
De officio pastoralis ("On the Pastoral Office") (Wycliffe), 121
denominationalism, 156
Desert Fathers, 32–33
Deus caritas est (Benedict XVI), 125
Devotio Moderna movement, 33
Dionysius, Saint, 105
divine, human and. *See* mystical dimension
"The Dogmatic Constitution on the Church in the Modern World" (Vatican II), 44
Dominic Guzman, Saint, 14
Donatist controversy, 35
Drane, John, 66

early ascetic movements, 135–36
Early Catholicism, 20
Eastern Christian spiritual life, 54–55
ecclesial shape, toward
    evangelical dimension, 18–21
    intellectual dimension, 92–93
    mystical dimension, 113–14
    pastoral dimension, 128–130
    Pentecostal dimension, 44–47
    prophetic dimension, 145–46
    scriptural dimension, 68–70
ecumenical movement, 147–48
Edict of Milan (313), 138
Education in Ancient Israel (Crenshaw), 72
Edwards, Bela Bates, 90
Edwards, Jonathan, 15, 88–89
Ely, Richard T., 139
Emergent Church movement, 17
encounter, of divine and human, 63
English Reformation, 58–59
Epiphany Church (Dallas/Fort Worth, TX), 68
The Epistle of Diognetus, 77
eschatological phase of sacred history, 62

INDEX

Eucharist, 51, 53, 59, 153
Eusebius of Caesarea, 137
Evagrius Ponticus, 80, 104
Evangelical Catholicism, 17–18
evangelical dimension
    characteristics, defining, 6–9
    in church history, 9–18
    ecclesial shape, toward, 18–21
    scriptural roots, 1–6
evangelical monks, 12–13
Evangelical *Ressourcement*, 67
Evangelical Revival, 15–16
Evangelicalism, contemporary trends in, 16–17, 127–28
Evangelicals and Catholics Together (document), 17
Evangelii gaudium (Francis, Pope), 18, 140
Evangelii nuntiandi (Paul VI), 18
evangelist, term usage, 6
"The Exciting Future of Evangelical Sacramentalism" (Penduck), 66–67
Exhortation to Martyrdom (Origen), 136

Falwell, Jerry, 16
Fénelon, François de Salignac de la Motte, 110
Fichte, Johann, 84
Fides et ratio (John Paul II), 86–88
First Great Awakening, 15–16
Fischer, Benjamin L., 121
former prophets, Old Testament, 132
forthtelling charism, 131, 134, 136
Fox, George, 36
Francis, Pope, 18, 125–26, 139–141
Francis de Sales, Saint, 123–24
Francis of Assisi, Saint, 14, 82
free church tradition, 150
fruits of the Spirit, 26
fundamentalist/fundamentalism, 16, 88–92, 148, 154–55

garment of skin, 104
George, Henry, 139
Gerson, John, 84
Gertrude the Great, 108

Gladden, Washington, 139
globalization, 148
God
    father, 1–2
    holiness of, 95–96
    Holy Spirit. *see* Holy Spirit
    image versus likeness, 104
    intimacy with, 95–97
    Kingdom of God, 62–63, 76, 139
    as love, 109
    as shepherd, 115–16
    son. *see* Jesus
    theophanic encounter with, 95
gospel, central understanding of, 3–4
grace of God, 14, 70
Graham, Billy, 16, 89
Grande, Rutilio, 143
Gregory III, Pope, 13
Gregory of Nazianzus, Saint, 31–32, 80
Gregory of Nyssa, Saint, 80, 95, 103–5
Gregory the Great, Saint (Pope), 13, 119–120
Groote, Geert, 84
Guéranger, Prosper, 59, 60
Guinness, Os, 88
Guyon, Jeanne-Marie Bouvier de la Motte, 110

Hadewijch of Antwerp, 108, 109
Hegel, Georg Wilhelm Friedrich, 84
Hildegard of Bingen, Saint, 107–10
Hofstadter, Richard, 89–91
Holy Spirit
    Basil of Caesars, Saint and, 31–32
    Gregory of Nazianzus, Saint and, 31–32
    Montanism and, 30–31
    movements of, 156
    pastoral leadership, 129
    presence of, 24–30
    . *See also* Charismatic Movement
Holy Theophany Orthodox Church (Colorado Springs, CO), 68
Hopkins, Gerard Manley, 64
human dignity, *Laudato si,'* 140
human intellect, 75–76, 87–88
Hus, Jan, 84
Hutton, E. F., 80

INDEX

hypocrites, intolerance of, 7, 154

Ignatius of Antioch, Saint, 9–10, 77
Ignatius of Loyola, Saint, 15
inculturation, 8
independent churches, 153
Innocent III, Pope, 126
institutional church, 150–51
integral approach to scripture reading, 71
integral church
   current shape of, 151–55
   institutional church, 150–51
   need for, 149–150
   shape of future, 155–56
   threats to, 148–49
   time has come for, 147–48
intellectual dimension
   characteristics, defining, 74–77
   in church history, 77–92
   ecclesial shape, toward, 92–93
   scriptural roots, 71–74
Introduction to the Devout Life (de Sales), 123
Irenaeus of Lyons, Saint, 56, 77
Irwin, Kevin W., 64–65

Jaeger, Werner, 103
Jansenists, 33
Jesuits, 15
Jesus
   evangelical dimension and, 7–9
   forthtelling charism, 134
   the Holy Spirit and, 24–25
   memory of in the Gospel message, 3–4
   Messianic fulfillment, 98
   Transfiguration of, 98
Jesus People movement, 18
Joachim of Fiore/Joachimism, 35–36
John, archbishop of Ravenna, 119
John Cassian, Saint, 80
John of Damascus, Saint, 55
John Paul II, Saint (Pope), 18, 86–88
John the Baptist, Saint, 5, 134
John the Evangelist, Saint, 109
John XII, Pope, 126
John XXIII, Pope, 125–26

justification, 14–15, 19
Justin Martyr, Saint, 77

Kant, Immanuel, 84
Keating, Anna, 68
Keble, John, 58–59
King, Martin Luther, Jr., 139, 141–43
King James Version of the Bible, 58–59
Kingdom of God, 62–63, 76, 139
Küng, Hans, 86

Lanfranc (monk), 81
Latin American Catholicism, 143
latter prophets, Old Testament, 132
Laudato si' (Francis, Pope), 139, 140–41
Leinsle, Ulrich, 84
Leo XIII, Saint (Pope), 60
Lérins Abbey, 12
Lewis, C. S., 89
liberalism, 148–49
"Liberation Spirituality" (Ashley), 144
liberation theology, 143–45
Life of Moses (Gregory of Nyssa), 95, 103
liturgical calendar, 70
Liturgical Movement, 59–61
Lombards, 120
Lord's Prayer, 139
love
   God as, 109
   mystical vision in, 104
   reason and, 109
Lubac, Henri de, 67
Lull, Raymond, 108
Luther, Martin, 8, 11, 14–15, 56
Lutheranism, 19, 37
Luxeuil Abbey, 13

Madame Guyon, 110
Maier, Martin, 144
major prophets, Old Testament, 132
Manichean, 90
Marcion, 75
Marguerite Porete, 108, 109, 110
Marmoutier Abbey, 12
marriage, sacrament of, 51
Mars Hill (Grand Rapids, MI), 68

INDEX

Martin of Tours, Saint, 12
martyrs, 9–10, 77, 135–36
Mary, Saint (mother of Jesus), 98–99, 108
Mary and Martha (disciples), 98–99
Mary Magdalene, Saint, 3
'McDonaldized' system, 66
McGinn, Bernard, 102
McLaren, Brian, 17
Mechtild of Magdeburg, 108
Meister Eckhart, 108
Mendicant Movements, 14
Merton, Thomas, 111–13, 138
Methodism, 38
Methodist movement, 58
Methodist Revival, 33, 41
Methodius, Saint, 13
Michel, Virgil, 60
minor prophets, Old Testament, 132
Missionaries of Charity, 124–25
missionary endeavors, 12–13
Molinos, Miguel de, 110
monastic guest houses, 154
monastic reform, 135–36
monasticism, 19, 111
monks, evangelical, 12–13
monotheistic tradition, 54–55
Mont César, 60
Montanus/Montanism, 30–31, 137
Moravians, 37–38
Moses, prophetic role, 133
Mother Teresa of Calcutta, Saint, 124–25
Motovilov, Nicholas, 39
mystical dimension
  characteristics, defining, 100–102
  in church history, 103–13
  ecclesial shape, toward, 113–14
  scriptural roots, 94–100
The Mystical Theology (Pseudo-Dionysius), 104
The Mysticism of Paul the Apostle (Schweizer), 33–34
mystics/mysticism, 33–34, 37, 78, 99, 154

Neoplatonism, 81
New Calvinism movement, 17

new evangelization, 18
New Life Church (Colorado Springs, CO), 68
New Prophecy, 30
New Testament
  evangelical dimension of the church, 2
  literary styles, 72–73
  mystical dimension, 96, 98–100
  pastoral dimension, 116–17
  Pentecostal dimension, 24–26
  period of, 35
  prophetic dimension, 134
  sacramental dimension, 51–52
The New Westminster Dictionary of Christian Spirituality, 144
Newman, John Henry, 58–59
Nobel Peace Prize, 37, 125
Noll, Mark, 88–90
non-liturgical churches, 154
North American Protestantism, 139
Nouvelle Théologie, 67

Old Testament
  evangelical dimension of the church, 1–6
  literary styles, 72
  mystical dimension, 94–98
  pastoral dimension, 115–16
  Pentecostal dimension, 22–24
  period of, 35
  prophetic dimension, 132–34
  sacramental dimension, 48–51
On First Principles (Origen), 78
"On the Pastoral Office" (*De officio pastoralis*) (Wycliffe), 121
oneness. of the church, 10
Order of the Visitation, 124
Origen of Alexandria, 76–77, 103, 104, 136
Orthodox Church, 152
Orthodoxy, 18, 39–40
Oxford Movement, 58–59, 67
Ozman, Agnes, 41

Parham, Charles, 40
Paschal Mystery, 4, 99
pastoral dimension

INDEX

characteristics, defining, 117–18
church history, 118–128
ecclesial shape, toward, 128–130
scriptural roots, 115–17
pastoral leadership, 127–28, 149
Patrick, Saint (Ireland), 12–13
Patristic Period, 76–77
Paul of Tarsus, Saint
   as Apostle to the Gentiles, 73
   on baptism, 51
   human intellect's role, 76–77
   justification and, 20
   mystical encounter, 99–100
   the Paschal Mystery and, 99
   on role of Holy Spirit, 26, 45
   theological presuppositions, 73–74, 79–80
   on understanding of gospel, 3–5
Paul VI, Pope, 18
Penduck, Joshua, 66–67
Pentecostal dimension
   characteristics, defining, 26–30
   in church history, 30–44
   current shape of, 153
   ecclesial shape, toward, 44–47
   scriptural roots, 22–26
Pentecostal fundamentalism, 16
Pentecostal prophecy, 136–37
Pentecostalism, twentieth century, 40–42, 127–28
personal salvation, 15–16
philosophy versus theology, 87
Pia Desideria (Spener), 37
Picts of Northern Scotland, 13
Pietists, 33, 36–37, 88
Pius IX, Pope, 126
Pius XII, Pope, 126
Plato, 67, 81, 106
Presbyterorum ordinis (Vatican II), 121
The Presence of God (McGinn), 102
pride, 106
priesthood
   characteristics befitting, 121–22
   illnesses plaguing, 122
   See also pastoral dimension
Progress and Poverty (George), 139
progressive side of church, 148–49
prophetic, term usage, 131

prophetic dimension
   characteristics, defining, 134–35
   church history, 135–145
   ecclesial shape, toward, 145–46
   monasticism period and, 19
   scriptural roots, 132–34
prophetic enthusiasm, 135–36
The Prophetic Imagination (Brueggemann), 132
prophets, role of, 115–16, 132–35, 133n4, 141
Protestant fundamentalism, 16
Protestant Reformation, 8, 14–15, 120–23
Protestantism, 152–53
Pseudo-Dionysius, 105–6
Puritans, 58
Pusey, Edward Bouverie, 58–59

Quakers, 36–37
Quietism, 110–11

Radical Reformation, 56–57
Rahner, Karl, 62–64
Rauschenbusch, Walter, 139
reason, love and, 109
Rerum Novarum (Leo XIII), 60, 139
revivals, 15–16, 33, 37, 41, 89–90
rhetoric of sacramentality, 64
Rite of Christian Initiation of Adults (RCIA), 61
Robertson, Pat, 16
Roman Catholic Church
   American Catholicism, 90–91
   Charismatic Renewal, 43–44
   Counter-Reformation, 120, 123
   English Reformation and, 58
   Evangelical Catholicism, 17–18
   Evangelii gaudium (Francis, Pope), 18
   Ignatius of Loyola's conversion, 15
   Laudato si' (Francis, Pope), 140
   Liturgical Movement, 59–61
   Luther on, 15
   Merton's conversion to, 111
   new evangelization, 18
   Order of the Visitation, 124
   popes. *see specific popes by name*

(Roman Catholic Church continued)
   Rite of Christian Initiation of Adults (RCIA), 61
   scandalous events, 127–28
   social justice, 112–13, 120, 139–140
   Vatican Council I, 87
   Vatican Council II. *see* Second Vatican Council
   . *See also* integral church
Romero, Oscar, Saint, 143, 145

sacramental, term usage, 48
sacramental dimension, 19
sacramental ontology, 67
sacramental theology, 61–62
"A Sacramental World–Sacramentality As The Primary Language for Sacraments" (Irwin), 64
sacramentalism, 154
sacramentality, 64–68
Sacred Scriptures, as sole authority for Christians, 14
Sacrosanctum concilium, 61, 62, 153
St. John's Abbey, 60
sanctification, 41, 69
scandal, 7
The Scandal of the Evangelical Mind (Noll), 88
scandalous events, in pastoral leadership, 127–28
Schillebeeckx, Edward, 62–64
Schleiermacher, Friedrich, 84–86
Schmemann, Alexander, 68–69
Scholasticism, 80–84
Schweizer, Albert, 99
Scivias (Hildegard), 108
scriptural dimension
   characteristics, defining, 52–54
   in church history, 54–68
   ecclesial shape, toward, 68–70
   scriptural roots, 48–52
scriptural roots
   Evangelical dimension, 1–6
   intellectual dimension, 71–74
   mystical dimension, 94–100
   pastoral dimension, 115–17
   Pentecostal dimension, 22–26
   prophetic dimension, 132–34

   sacramental dimension, 48–52
Second Vatican Council
   Catholic Charismatic Renewal, 43–44
   Constitution on the Sacred Liturgy, 61–62
   "The Dogmatic Constitution on the Church in the Modern World," 44
   on evangelicals and Roman Catholics, 17–18, 67
   fundamentalistic trend, 91–92
   integration of ecclesial dimensions, 152
   Liturgical Movement, 59
   Presbyterorum ordinis, 121
   renewal of sacramental dimension, 152
   universal call to holiness, 123
secularization, 151, 155
Seraphim of Sarov, Saint, 38–40
Seventh Ecumenical Council (787), 55
Seymour, William J., 41
shepherd, God as, 115–17
single tax movement, 139, 139n6
Sisters of Loreto, 124
Sobrino, Jon, 143
social gospels, 139–141
social justice, 112–13, 120
social justice, *Laudato si,'* 140
Society of Friends (Quakers), 36–37
Sojourners movement, 16–17
solidarity, *Laudato si,'* 140
Song of Songs, 97, 101, 103–5, 106–7
Soul, description of, 110
Spener, Philipp Jakob, 37
Spiritual Exercises (Ignatius of Loyola), 15
spiritual gifts (charisms), 26, 43
static triumphalism, 132–33
Stewart, Carlyle Fielding, III, 141–42
Strong, Josiah, 139
subsidiarity, *Laudato si,'* 140
Summa Theologiae (Aquinas), 82
Swedish, Margaret, 143
Symeon the New Theologian Saint, 33–35

Teresa of Avila, Saint, 110

INDEX

Teresa of Calcutta, Saint, 124–25
Tertullian, 10, 30–31, 77–78
Theodore the Studite, 55, 56
theology
    driving force of the New Testament, 72–73
    philosophy versus, 87
    sacramental, 61–62
Theology of the Old Testament (Breuggemann), 50
A Theology of the Social Gospel, (Rauschenbusch), 139
theophanic encounter with God, 94–95, 98–99
Thérèse of Lisieux, Saint, 124
Thomas Aquinas, Saint, 35, 63, 80–84
Thompson, Joseph Milburn, 141n10
The Tracts for the Times (Church of England), 58
traditionalism, 148
Treatise on the Love of God (de Sales), 123
Trinity, 31–32, 43, 69

Vatican Council I, 87
Vatican Council II. *See* Second Vatican Council

The Village Church (Flower Mound, TX), 68
von Balthasar, Hans Urs, 86

Wallis, Jim, 16–17
Weigel, George, 17–18
Wesley, Charles, 37, 58
Wesley, John, 15, 37–38, 58
Whitefield, George, 15
"Why Evangelical Megachurches are Embracing (Some) Catholic Traditions" (Keating), 68
Williams, A. N., 78
Willow Creek (Chicago, IL), 68
Wisdom, of the Spirit, 24, 27
Wisdom of God, 101
Wisdom of Solomon, 97
Word, liturgy of the, 68–69
Word of God, term usage, 7
Wyclif, John, 120–23
Wycliffe, John, 84

Zen Buddhism, 113
Zwingli, Ulrich, 56

www.ingramcontent.com/pod-product-compliance
Lightning Source LLC
Chambersburg PA
CBHW051056160426
43193CB00010B/1212